ECONOMIC ISSUES, PROBLEMS

LABOR MARKETS

POLICIES, CHALLENGES
AND THE ROLE OF GLOBALIZATION

ECONOMIC ISSUES, PROBLEMS AND PERSPECTIVES

ECONOMIC ISSUES, PROBLEMS AND PERSPECTIVES

LABOR MARKETS

POLICIES, CHALLENGES
AND THE ROLE OF GLOBALIZATION

WILLIAM E. GROSSMAN
EDITOR

New York

NOTICE TO THE READER

The Publisher has taken reasonable care in the preparation of this book, but makes no expressed or implied warranty of any kind and assumes no responsibility for any errors or omissions. No liability is assumed for incidental or consequential damages in connection with or arising out of information contained in this book. The Publisher shall not be liable for any special, consequential, or exemplary damages resulting, in whole or in part, from the readers' use of, or reliance upon, this material. Any parts of this book based on government reports are so indicated and copyright is claimed for those parts to the extent applicable to compilations of such works.

Independent verification should be sought for any data, advice or recommendations contained in this book. In addition, no responsibility is assumed by the publisher for any injury and/or damage to persons or property arising from any methods, products, instructions, ideas or otherwise contained in this publication.

This publication is designed to provide accurate and authoritative information with regard to the subject matter covered herein. It is sold with the clear understanding that the Publisher is not engaged in rendering legal or any other professional services. If legal or any other expert assistance is required, the services of a competent person should be sought. FROM A DECLARATION OF PARTICIPANTS JOINTLY ADOPTED BY A COMMITTEE OF THE AMERICAN BAR ASSOCIATION AND A COMMITTEE OF PUBLISHERS.

Additional color graphics may be available in the e-book version of this book.

Library of Congress Cataloging-in-Publication Data

ISBN: 978-1-62948-662-8

Labor markets : policies, challenges and the role of globalization / editor, William E. Grossman.
pages cm
Includes index.
Labor market. 2. Labor. 3. Labor policy. I. Grossman, William E.
HD5706.L2186 2014
331.12--dc23
                              2013045186

Published by Nova Science Publishers, Inc. † New York

CONTENTS

Preface   vii

Chapter 1   Does Education Matter? A Regression and Factorial
                  Analysis between Work and Education   1
                  Carla Silva

Chapter 2   A Lingering Decline or a Stable Future?
                  The Case for Investing in Rural Tourism   35
                  Gordon B. Cooke, Jennifer K. Burns
                  and Kyle W. J. Vardy

Chapter 3   Challenging Globalization: An Extension
                  of a Theory of Marginality Utilizing the Case
                  of Public School Teachers in the
                  Dominican Republic   63
                  Karie Jo Peralta and George Wilson

Chapter 4   "Learning a Living"? European Union Lifelong
                  Learning Policy: Advocating for "Employability"   85
                  Eugenia A. Panitsides, MSc., PhD.

Index   103

PREFACE

In this book, the authors present topical research in the study of labor market policies, challenges and its role in globalization. Topics discussed include work values and educational sociodemographics from a sample of young people in vocational education in Barcelona, Spain; the economic restructuring of rural communities through rural tourism; challenging globalization and a theory of marginality using the case of public school teachers in the Dominican Republic; and a review of the development of comprehensive lifelong learning strategies in enhancing employment, combating unemployment and increasing competitiveness in the European Union.

Chapter 1 – This chapter is part of a doctoral research, which is based on a questionnaire on work values and educational sociodemographic from a sample of young people in vocational education in Barcelona in 2012. It is intended to show the different relationships between work and education in the young professional middle and upper cycles through factor analysis of the dimensions analyzed. Thus demonstrating a linear regression between the variable "work" and "satisfaction", the author developed a theoretical analysis of the trajectory of the concept of work for these young people. In the first part of this chapter analyzes the theoretical construct of this analysis by discussing the concept of social and cultural capital and habitus and its importance in the difference between classes. The inclusion to work, to education and training are human rights, and are key requirements for access to employment, subject to a "knowledge society" in a broad context of globalization. There is no longer a job without proper training, and in turn, a respected work includes appropriate training, qualification and an update. Education and training are part of this form, an economic response but also social, in a globalized world.

The difference between the middle classes and upper classes is accentuated particularly in education postsecondary and university education system. The origin of speech is not individual, reveals a socio-historical position, taking as reference the interaction and conflict between different social groups. In the second part of this chapter is intended to describe the variables selected for the study, performing the inferential analysis, describing the sample and methodology used for the research in question.

Chapter 2- Partially due to the effects of globalization, rural communities within industrialized nations have had to endure economic restructuring as manufacturing and traditional industries such as small-scale fishing or farming have been replaced by service industry-based economies. One could argue that it is important to differentiate between near-rural (or suburban) communities and more remote, truly 'rural' communities. In the latter, where individuals cannot commute for daily work to an urban center, populations tend to be declining, at least on a relative basis. For these rural communities to remain vibrant, many will need to embrace new industries as a means of maintaining employment and economic activity. Using two examples from the Canadian province of Newfoundland and Labrador, you could argue for the investment of public funds to try to sustain rural communities by boosting tourism visitors, and hence, revenues and employment. Industrialized nations like Canada have seen a growing 'casualization' of jobs in the labor market, and this trend is often accentuated in rural communities where unemployment tends to be higher, and seasonal employment is prevalent. Tourism, and certainly rural tourism, is also very likely to be a seasonal exercise, and as such, it can be argued that it generates only poor quality jobs. This could be viewed from a different angle. Developing a seasonal tourism industry in a rural area can be a way to provide a level of economic sustainability, but without undermining local historical, social, and cultural norms and activities. In fact, if public funds are used to improve and expand rural infrastructure and the number of events and activities, then visitors and local citizens both benefit, especially when those events and activities revive or maintain local traditions. Moreover, the seasonal and/or part-time jobs created by tourism potentially fit the needs of older rural individuals, while also providing opportunities for local entrepreneurs once public funds have created sufficient tourist activity. Some would view this approach as being far more desirable than doing nothing while rural communities try to cope with economic restructuring and declining populations. That said, developing a tourism industry requires ongoing, significant capital investments to create a critical mass of attractions and events, and even then, someone, or some group, within the community needs to champion the cause. While developing tourism is expensive and time-consuming and the prospects for success are far from guaranteed, the question remains, if not tourism, then what policy alternatives offer better prospects?

Chapter 3 - This chapter builds on Torres's (2009) theory of "marginality" in understanding how socioeconomic inequality generated by a neoliberal form of globalization can be challenged and ultimately, more equitable outcomes can ensue. Specifically, based on extensive field work in which you utilize teachers' struggle in the Dominican Republic for better livelihoods, then add three tenets to Torres' theory: (1) Pursuing social transformation requires the incorporation of the poor; (2) The marginalized are responsible for integrating others who are socially excluded in transformative social justice learning practices; and, (3) The marginalized have the ability to initiate the creation of a world free of social inequalities, that, when viewed through the lens of a "transformative social justice learning" rationale moves forward an agenda that provides a more equitable outcome from globalization processes and conclude, by discussing how this critical agenda can be further developed in subsequent research.

Chapter 4 - In the post-industrial context, investment in Lifelong Learning (LLL) has undoubtedly been acknowledged as a conditio sine qua non for sustainable growth and social stability. Especially within the European Union (EU), since the 1990s, LLL has been regarded as a strategic parameter for building the "most competitive economy in the world based on knowledge". In this context ensuring continual adaptability and employability of the work force, particularly the most vulnerable, and combating skills mismatches, have been among main objectives of EU LLL policy to tackle the challenges emerging from increasing competitiveness in the global market, development of information and communication technologies, the Union enlargement, as well as demographic ageing. The present chapter aims to critically review the development of comprehensive LLL strategies in enhancing employment, combating unemployment and increasing competitiveness of the EU. Given the aims of the study, Critical Discourse Analysis (Fairclough, 1993) has been employed, systematically exploring relationships of causality between discursive practice and wider social structures and processes. Through an interpretative approach of the political discourse, it sought to define trends and identify interrelations between EU LLL strategies and emerging challenges within the Union, as well as global socio-economic mandates.

Findings indicated that high unemployment rates during the mid 1990s led to a rhetoric shift replacing "employment" with "employability", whilst rising global competitiveness and economic crisis in 2008 have brought "flexicurity" to the fore. Hence, LLL has been assigned a strategic role in providing for an "up-to-date" workforce, with a better skills match considered "flexible" enough to adapt to changing labor demands, so as to enable EU remain a strong global actor.

In: Labor Markets
Editor: William E. Grossman

ISBN: 978-1-62948-662-8
© 2014 Nova Science Publishers, Inc.

Chapter 1

DOES EDUCATION MATTER? A REGRESSION AND FACTORIAL ANALYSIS BETWEEN WORK AND EDUCATION

*Carla Silva**

Autonoma University of Barcelona, Faculty of Politic science, Spain
Lusophona University of Lisbon, Faculty of Education Police, Portugal

ABSTRACT

This chapter is part of a doctoral research, which is based on a questionnaire on work values and educational sociodemographic from a sample of young people in vocational education in Barcelona in 2012. It is intended to show the different relationships between work and education in the young professional middle and upper cycles through factor analysis of the dimensions analyzed. Thus demonstrating a linear regression between the variable "work" and "satisfaction", we have developed a theoretical analysis of the trajectory of the concept of work for these young people. In the first part of this chapter analyzes the theoretical construct of this analysis by discussing the concept of social and cultural capital and habitus and its importance in the difference between classes. The inclusion to work, to education and training are human rights, and are key requirements for access to employment, subject to a "knowledge society" in a broad context of globalization.

* Corresponding author: Carla Silva, E-mail: silvacarla.uab@gmail.com.

There is no longer a job without proper training, and in turn, a respected work includes appropriate training, qualification and an update. Education and training are part of this form, an economic response but also social, in a globalized world. The difference between the middle classes and upper classes is accentuated particularly in education postsecondary and university education system. The origin of speech is not individual, reveals a socio-historical position, taking as reference the interaction and conflict between different social groups. In the second part of this chapter is intended to describe the variables selected for the study, performing the inferential analysis, describing the sample and methodology used for the research in question.

Keywords: Human capital, social and cultural capital, professional education, habitus and social reproduction, factor analysis

1. INTRODUCTION

Education is receptor of the influence socio-historical sociology of education that aims to explain. From a global perspective, political, economic, demographic, technological and religious, all have an influence on education so that, according Horcajo (1976, 1991), the education system is a microcosm of society itself. The system adjusts to the social limitations and resources that it provides. The education system will then be a reflection of the global system itself.

In Marxist conception, the form of action and experience that distinguishes the human species is the work, because education is a process that identifies itself as the modeling of the mind of each individual through the socialization. The education in this guideline is more distinct and higher than the simple instruction. In biological conception labor as an organized society, does not distinguish the human species from other species. Attentive, for example, the family Formicidae, to which belong the ants, or family Apicidae, to which belong the bees we know so well. In these species, the work is the social position that binds the society to which they belong, whilst in the human species is a social position that represents the work that connects us to the society we have built. So, over the ages, the concept of work and its relationship to society progressed with the evolution of the human species itself. The work became historically and its educational function always depends on specific socio-economic conditions of the culture in which man produces and develops their life and interests (Hinojal, 1980).

The inclusion to work, to education and training, and human rights are key requirements for access to employment, respected by a "knowledge society", in a broad context of regionalization and globalization technologization.

There is no longer a job without proper training, and in turn a respected work includes adequate training, qualification and an upgrade. In 2008, the European Community states that it should be give credibility to and should invest more in human capital, so that we can achieve the development of European society, "investing more and more effectively in human capital and creativity throughout people's lives are crucial conditions for Europe's success in a globalised world" (CE, 2008)[1].

Navas, Martinez e Gomez (2004), refer that family conditions and socio-economic conditions are important constraints and key in which young people realize their paths and making decisions, shall face continuing studies, depending always on the social habitus. However, for Sierra (2001) socializing the young in the values of the labor market through the education system is an action taken outside the school perimeter, depending on policies of different power groups and local government.

Through policy LOGSE (Organic law for the education system), along with the increase in unemployment, vocational guidance has taken a direction with some priority. Notwithstanding this, it should be taken into consideration that according to this author, there is a contradiction of the political focus - economic hegemony, in which young people are seen like mere elements of the production system in the market.

In this chapter, we intend to underline the importance given to the work, by a socio-demographic analysis of young people in vocational education. These young people are confronted with a social and cultural capital, in a social space of symbolic violence, where for selection by a phenomenon of Social Darwinism; those who have a high innate capital survive, and ensure their posterity, by cultural reproduction.

It is demonstrated differences in labor relations and education in these young people, and through factor analysis of the dimensions analyzed, builds up a table of linear regression between the value given to work and satisfaction in vocational education. At the end of the chapter, we intend to demonstrate a theoretical trajectory analysis of the concept of work for these young people, take along this chapter as the dependent variable.

---

[1] In its conclusions of 22 May 2008, relating to education and training of adults (OJ C 140, 6.6.2008, p. 10.) The European Council recognizes the crucial role that they can play in achieving the goals of the Lisbon Strategy.

1.1. The Fallacy of Vocational Training

In Spain, as we know, develops vocational education in two cycles, the CFGM (Medium Cycles of Training Graduated) and the CFGS (Higher Cycles of Training Graduated), in close coordination with general education, being associated with a perspective of "transport", oriented to a continuation of studies, relating more the University to the higher cycle (CFGS), and the medium cycle (CFGM) to the labor market. The differences between these two types of training programs and social distinctions, that fall upon them differ greatly and are responsible for the enormous diversity of flows in social search.

The control of public schools is a form of political domination of the bourgeoisie and the liberal policy, it is an education policy class. According to Mir (1990), education results from work and preparation for work, in the Marxist line man is a social product of culture. For Bourdieu and Passeron (1977), the class struggle is always unequal, depending on where the cultural capital and class ethos stands. Students enter school with a cultural capital unequal, depending on their social background. The school distributes unevenly in cultural capital, with the aim of reproducing social stratification leading to a habitus.

Bourdieu (1983, 1992) and Bernstein (1996), understand the functionalism of the educational system, by how it exerts cultural transmission. School is not an institution to give opportunities to young people, but a space of struggle between groups that provides status, power and social differentiation.

To Baudelot and Establet (1998), the school work as a function used by the upper class to ensure your domain and class reproduction. From statistical studies, they show how the dropout is related to different social classes. The first part of education (lower secondary), is more connected to the labor market and the second part (upper secondary), gives access to a social prestige, as Schultz in 1968 defended his theory of human capital.

In Spain, the formation of CFGM gives access to a sector of the labor market, with less prestige and lower pay and CFGS allows access to culture and prestige of the best professions. This sets up a practice of structuralism Marxism, a principle of correspondence between the organizations, school practices and needs concrete reproduction of the social division of labor (Bonal, 2000).

By these words, it is understandable that sets a new world order, and there is a proposal for education, shaping the field of educational policies, which are now part of the transnational projects (Teodoro, 2008).

The field of education is linked to the interdependence of the fields of economy and society. Therefore, exits a proceeding of change that has enabled sharp differences in the various educational systems of each country. This hypothesis, admits that states are faced with questions coming, either by the process of transnational organization, whether the situation of the state in the same case (Antunes, 2004b).

These issues and pressures put State itself, in a situation of impaired options against the educational process. Given these observations, the State cannot fail to have their autonomy, but the guidelines will take you to make decisions and implement measures that arise following interpretations of institutions at the global level (Antunes 2004 a, b). Therefore, the most relevant effects of globalization are always based on the mode of regulation of the function and role of the state in the face of such phenomena, formalizing an agenda, ".... refers to the set of tensions and contradictions characteristic of the role of the state in democratic and capitalist societies." (Antunes, 2001, p. 167). Global and transnational policies do not come in our social and economic sphere in a balanced way, not by passive diffusion, it incurring processes that require active transport always precious by energy exchange. These exchanges are considered binding a change of habitat, thus not respect the balance of the medium and can thus lead to a state of social analysis. As said by Bonal and Rambla (2003), the neoliberal theories served as a form of analysis for the modification of educational practices, and ultimately as a narrative discourse. The government now became the mode of regulation of supranational institutions, and their influence on education has been evident for the past 30 years. All national policy frameworks are now shaped and delimited by these synergies within supranational institutions. It is from these external policies and its mode of regulation that can be seen the most obvious effects of globalization on the state (Dale, 2004). The education itself is linked to the concept of change and social reproduction. The society transformations have designed the role of the school throughout the ages. Enguita (1985b) shows the evolution of the role of education from industrial societies as well as their role in the current scenario.

The mass schooling was possible for everyone, delineated by an education with new strategies, applied in society over the historicity of a global Europe. The rise of private schools was one of these strategies to preserve the symbolic capital (ethos, style) through the conversion of economic capital, which ensures the rule of group or ruling class (Bourdieu, 1992). Schools are binding on the habitus of the ruling class as a natural and teach all young people, as if everyone had the same cultural habitus.

Thus, the dominant habitus is transformed into cultural capital that schools accept and take for granted, and that acts as a filter in society through a process of social hierarchy.

Some authors such as Garcia (2008) and Iregui (2002) argue that young people are reinforced with a cultural capital. However, there are young people who do not have this cultural capital, making it difficult to achieve success. This is presented as an operating strategy in schools. Is necessary or appropriate cultural capital acquired by assimilation to achieve success. The schools work according to a certain habitus, a habitus dominant, but also react to social changes (economic, technological and political). These perceptions, and are recognized in the field of school are at the same time by the same habitus dominant filtered.

1.2. Habitus and Capital - A Form of to Survive

However, Bourdieu refers to the importance of cultural capital through family and social background, as a form of reproduction of the education system, which are more important than production. By using the principle habitus as moderator, we infer itineraries and strategies, rather than simple theories of reproduction.

Therefore, in the labor market, the value of diplomas and credential is primarily a function of social and economic capital who owns them, and not by their overall value. The dominant groups legitimize concepts, which are more socially valued, and these cultural meanings are what, their local school chooses and selects, and within this dynamic, the possibilities of social mobility is based on a symbolic capital (Bourdieu, 1984).

The concept of cultural capital, referring to cultural and linguistic competence socially inherited, enables analyze its uneven distribution among social groups and school. To enable a particular curriculum, and to valuing a kind of cultural capital, it reproduces a type of social inequality.

It is necessary to promote policies that may lead to a higher demand and acceptance of these training modalities, and make adjustments is now a political and social demand.

Silva (2012B), showed that the inherited capital is a capital played. The author found, that the educational formations achievement of parents influences the vocational training in these training cycles in Barcelona. In this analysis Silva, explains that young people trained in CFGS, feel more motivated to work and seek employment and reaches the intended to work.

Also notes, that young people trained in CFGS can more often, find a significant work with contract, contrary to the cases of young graduates in CFGM, who have fewer expectations regarding to the future. The analysis gives a project of organizing society, because "those that contain an inherited high cultural capital mark the conversion of cultural capital in educational capital".

The labor market in most developed countries is characterized by high rates of youth unemployment, however investment in education and training by this population, is increasing. In both cases, may lead to a social error, generating a social and educational misfit, because the outcomes of both cycles are different.

1.3. The Importance of Degree and Work

The opportunities given by these two cycles and the expected opportunities in the labor market, linked to these two cycles graduation, show how equality of education is impossible. If we consider this, if all have finished their training, with the same qualifications, there would be no differentiation at work, and it must exist.

Is through this, which is form and binds the habitus inherent to social status. It is in school, that gets to select the qualifications and any attempt to delay this selection is a delay in entering the labor market (Brown, 2003). This is an understanding coded by globalization. So far, education and the labor market were contextualized to a national level, but now, there are currently transnational forces that shape the laws of the market and education and training.

The conversion of economic capital in educational capital is, according to Bourdieu (1988), a strategy that allows the class to maintain its position by their heirs. Thereby allowing the appropriation of the benefits of capital with increasing cultural capital, brought about by the translation structure of opportunities for access to the education system, are bound by a dialectical relationship with an elevation of cultural capital. We formulated in this way, a symbolic equation that intends to structure the space of symbolic action as an algorithm of the field.

This strategy can be calculated through the integral cultural capital innate (CCI), to the cultural capital acquired (CCA), from the matrix volume of Capital (VC) with the capital structure of the individual (EC), by the variance the time traveled (Δt), exponentiated to their habitus:

$$f(SE) = \log[space(pratice)] = \sum_{n=CCI}^{CCA} \left| \frac{(vc + ec)}{\Delta t} \right|^{habitus}$$

Therefore, the function of the educational system, F (SE), is viewed always by the sum of the aspirations, opportunities and social identity of the individual, into the educational system with the social identity in the labor market, which is expected, and that indeed, is obtained:

$$<=> f(SE) = \sum_{in\ the\ SE}^{out\ of\ the\ SE} (aspirations + opportunity$$
$$+\ social\ identity\ of\ the\ individual)$$
$$+\ social\ identity\ in\ the\ labor\ market$$

This process leads to a social maladjustment and an educational failure. With a high cultural capital valued by the educational system, it is possible to achieve certain titles in the labor market, which are highly requested, thereby obtaining an education return:

$$<=> f(SE) =$$
$social$ (mal)adjustment $+$ social identity in the labor market

$$<=> f(SE) = School\ Failure\ V\ f(SE) = Educational\ Achievement$$

The title, accredited by diploma intended to represent the educational experience, meaning therefore acquired knowledge but also justifies the skills, giving the employer a means to justify the ends. But this labor market, working conditions and provides social status in different jobs. Many young people enter the labor market with social disadvantages, believed by a diploma which initially gave them an opportunity (Brown, 2003).

The middle classes have adopted various strategies to ensure social position, that they can provide a quality of life. However, as they get improves conditions of access to different courses, worsens the conditions of the workspace labor, redefining itself to a cultural reproduction. Success is accredited by the inclusion and devalued by exclusion. Silva (2012a) argues that in the entry of professional training cycles in Barcelona, young people are faced with a requirement that is already generating class differentiation.

Those who are more motivated to work, are those who belongs to the middle training cycles, and higher degree, holders the best professions with better yields. Perales (2008) portrays us, how the school is used to maintain the function of reproduction of production relations. For this author, it is the school that forms the agents exploration and exploited in order to maintain the capitalist system.

For Christian Baudelot and Roger Establet (1976), the school is an instrument to the service of a dominant class, whose only purpose is to reproduce the relations of production and consequently the domination of the capitalist system. On the one hand, reproduces the social division that is produced later in the working world. According Perales (2008), the school fulfills another function - to display the structure of class relations.

With a high cultural capital valued by the education system, it is possible to achieve certain titles in the labor market that are highly requested, so you can keep or exceed the economic position (Bourdieu and Passeron, 1977).

The social space is constructed so that the groups are distributed according to their position (economic and social capital). The social will be closer to each other, since the groups have between themselves and similar points will be removed if the groups were further separated. Social space will be closer to each other, since the groups have between themselves similar points, and will be away from each ether, if the groups were separated. The space of social positions reflected in the space-making positions through the habitus. The position of each class of habitus is the product of social condition associated with a particular condition. It corresponds to a systematic set of assets and properties together by a purpose. The habitus is the principle generating and unifying, reflecting the intrinsic and relational position of a lifestyle, goods and practices. Putting focus on the principles of differentiation, the habitus is the generating element of practice and key factor of cultural or symbolic reproduction (Bourdieu, 1983).

The general secondary education describes the information linked to preparation for the pursuit of post-secondary education and higher, which includes a variety of pathways. Describes this, the most common academic courses in secondary education of traditional school, are connected to the labor market. However, education called "general" (Model School) was always linked in secondary, to preparation for pursuing higher studies, and vocational education (Dual Model and Non-Formal) always assigned the task of preparing for job. The expansion of university education is associated with the concept of inflation as the economic capital is greater than the cost of resources, this leads to an increase in these resources.

If young people is seeking certified qualifications, in universities and vocational training for certain jobs, and if the number of positions before these professions do not increase demand, inflation occurs, emerging a more qualified society (Brown, 2003). Having a social descension, the young are forced to go back to school to take other specializations, promoting those who contain an innate high capital, whether is cultural or economic, and these leads to a possibility to enter the labor market. The diploma is not in the hands of the acquired capital, but in the hand of the innate capital.

2. METHODOLOGY

2.1. Description of the Sample

The items of the questionnaire include dimensions that must be measured and check their conceptual relationships. The study of the psychometric properties of our instrument, namely the internal consistency was calculated by estimating the Cronbach's alpha internal reliability among items in each dimension and inter-items of the same size. Cronbach's alpha, has the important advantage of providing an outcome equal to the average of all possible bipartition coefficients with a given set of items. Hill and hill (2002) by referring to measure a latent variable "defined by a set of other variables" say that this is reliable if it is consistent" (pp. 141-142).

The alpha value of the whole questionnaire was $\alpha = 0.725$. With respect to construct validity, we used factor analysis by maximum likelihood, since this is one of the most used techniques to identify constructs underlying the results. Construct validity allows us to know, from the results in an instrument, if we can find one or more theoretical constructs of variables to evaluate the scale.

Assuming that the intercorrelations between the items can be explained by a smaller set of factors, which represent relationships among sets of interrelated variables, it will look through factor analysis to verify the internal validity of the instrument, trying to find an explanation for the variance of the results, resorting to the help of such independent components, obtained from the original variables.

One of the criteria for adequacy to perform the principal components analysis was given by the Bartlett's test of sphericity, which allows us to know if all the correlations in the matrix is different from zero. Bartlett's test has an associated significance level of less than $p < .05$, which leads to rejection of the hypothesis of correlation matrix of the population being the identity matrix (with determinant equal to 1), indicating that there are correlations between the variables. The value of chi-square is 5334.995, p <.001, and the Kaiser-Meyer-Olkin (KMO), which compares simple correlations with partial correlations observed in the variable, has a value of 0.769 for the questionnaire conducted.

After analysis of the internal consistency of the questionnaire, compared to values of alphas found, this is an instrument with good fidelity, since the category "aspects of life and aspects of training" presents an internal consistency of 0.808 and the category "course educational attraction in job" and "satisfaction" presents 0,798. In all vocational students of professional courses selected, were achieved in a total of 320 schools in 12 schools and 14 courses. The young people in our sample are mostly male gender, 89.38% and 10.53% of females. The average age is between 20 years to 24 years, representing 18.1% and 19.45% of the sample.

2.2. Study of the Variables

At this point, we tried to verify whether the average age is different in kind and frequency of education degree. For this, we apply the parametric One Way ANOVA test, and we intend to compare their average with 4 independent population groups, defined by a qualitative variable (independent - level of education and gender, gender CGF). The variable – genderCFG, is a variable of the transposed variables gender and level of education, and takes with code 1 - woman attending professional middle grade, 2 - man attending professional middle grade, 3 - women attending professional higher grade and 4 - man attending professional higher grade.

In the figure I, we can observed the four samples are taken from normally distributed populations, the age follows a normal distribution in the population of young men attending the middle and upper cycle, and so it as the population of young women attending the middle and upper cycle, then the samples are independent. The samples are not related to each other, therefore is verified the assumption of independence. The value of Levene $(3, 316) = 1.462$, p-value = $0.225 > \alpha = 0.05$, so we accept the null hypothesis of equality of variances. The assumption of the variance is calculated, so we can apply the test parametric one-way ANOVA.

Since p-value = $0.311 > \alpha = 0.05$ then null hypothesis is not rejected, there is no statistical evidence that the mean age among young people, is different between 4 degrees of training and gender $(F (3,319) = 1.196$, p-value = 0.311), therefore the average age is no different in professional degrees.

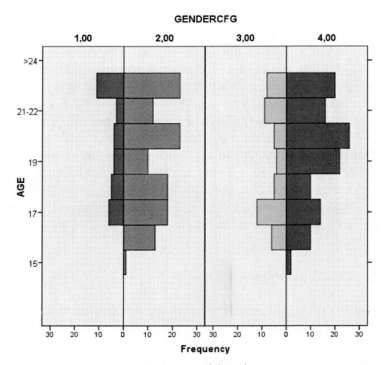

Font: own elaboration.

Figure 1. Study of the distribution of age by gender and grade (GENDERCFG).

Figure II reveals that young people have an average age between 19 and 20 years. The lowest average age (19 years), belongs to the young females attending the higher professional grade, and the highest average (20 years), belongs to the young females attending medium professional grade.

We can see that the frequency of education, is higher in young people who attend school in higher graduations (3 and 4), while the young people who attend the middle graduation are older. This enters into agreement with the literature review, made in the first part of this chapter, we argue that the middle grade is more stigmatized in society, because, it was an educational pathway for young people who could not reach the pathway general education, and in this way can reach other studies. Through the intersection of variables, we can observe with a significance level of less than $\alpha=0.0005$, the value of chi-square Person is 11,133. This means that not only these variables are related, as expected, we can find a value of α^2 of 11,133 or more less, than five times in every 10,000 in population.

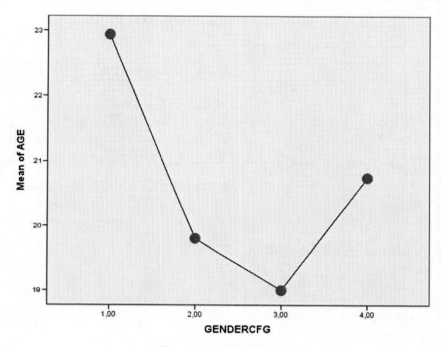

Font: own elaboration.

Figure II. Study of the distribution of mean age by gender and grade (GENDERCFG).

So we can say with some certainty that students studying in the higher grade are younger, inquiring by this fact, the average cycle is a graduation alternative for youth with failure.

It seems important to verify whether the variables stroke frequency, education degree and gender with education degree, are independent variables of nationality and the nationality of the parents. For a significance level of 0.05, as can be seen in Table I, there is statistical evidence for the claim that all variables (CFGMCFGS, generoCFG and Stroke) are not independent variables nationality and nationality of the parents. And, by Cramer's V test, we can say that the variables are related.

We can observe from Figure II that the average for young women in the higher degree (3), is represented by young Spanish nationality, as opposed to young people of another nationality (2, Young males attending the middle degree), showing that nationality influences the frequency of studies.

Carla Silva

Table 1. Study on the independence of the variables

Matriz_crosstab			
	CFGMCGFS	GenderCFG	COURSE
NATIONALITY OF FATHER			
x^2	(1)12,657	(3)13,811	(3)33,455
p-value**	0,000	0,03	0,01
(Cramer's V)	0,199	0,208	0,323
Exact Sig+	0,000	0,03	0.01
NATIONALITY OF MOTHER			
x^2	(1)8,524	(3)9,625	(3)22,986
p-value**	0,03	0,022	0,042
(Cramer's V)	0,163	0,173	0,268
Exact Sig*	0,04	0,022	0,042
NATIONALITY OF YOUNG			
x^2	(13)6,192	(3)9,059	(1)26,323
p-value**	0,01	0,029	0,015
(Cramer's V)	0,139	0,168	0,287
Exact Sig*	0,013	0,029	0,015

Font: own elaboration.
*With p-value<α=0,05, rejects the null hypothesis.
**pvalue<α=0,05, for n<20, with the exact p-value.

There is statistical evidence to affirm that the qualifications of the parents in this sample is representative of the population, as there are no significant differences between observed and what is known of the population, with the qualifications of the mother is (α^2 (6) = 0.947, p-value = 0.987) [2], and for the qualifications of the father ($\alpha^2(6)$ = 9.161, p-value = 0.165) [2]. This ensures the representativeness of the sample to the qualifications of the parents.

It seems important at this point to reflect about the possible influence that the qualifications of the parents may have in the choice of courses for children. The data evidences and allows us to understand, if the variables "qualification of parents" and "course" and "degree of training" and variables "degree training with gender" are independent. To do this, we must apply the test of independence chi-square (Laureano, 2011).

In this sample, for a significance level of 0.05, there is statistical evidence to affirm that the qualifications of parents and choice of degree course are related.

For the relationship between the variable "qualification of the parent" and choice of "course", there was the nonexistence of independence between the characteristics (α^2 (78) = 135.537, p-value is approximately zero), and the relationship between "qualification" and "education degree" (α^2 (6) = 12.715, p-value = 0.048), and finally between the "qualifications parent", "gender and course" (α^2 (18) = 47.440, p-value = 0), for all values Sig <0, 05, then reject the null hypothesis which says that the variables are independent, because it turns out that the variables are related. We had the same procedure for the qualification of the mother and, it was found that the variables qualification and choice of course relate to each other with (α^2 (78) = 118.978, p-value is approximately zero), and the variables and qualification education degree with gender, relate to each other (α^2 (18) = 29.75, p-value = .04). But for the variable education degree and qualification, the variables do not seem to be dependent (α^2 (6) = 8.663, p-value = 0.193), as this relationship p-value > 0.05, supports the hypothesis independence of variables.

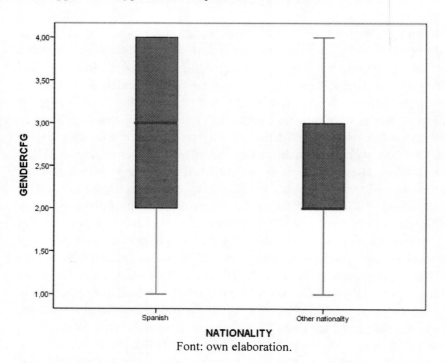

NATIONALITY
Font: own elaboration.

Figure III. Study of the average frequency of professional degrees, by nationality.

**Table 2. Study on the relationship between independence
and the variables studied in Barcelona**

Matriz_crosstab_Barcelona			
	CFGMCGFS	genderCFG	Course
Father qualification (Cramer's V)	0,199	0,222	0,266
Exact Sig	0,048	0,000	0,000
Mother qualification (Cramer's V)	0,165	0,176	0,249
Exact Sig	0,193	0,04	0,02

Font: own elaboration.

To understand to what extent there is a relationship of dependence on the variables, we can apply a nonparametric test for nominal qualitative variables. To infer relationships between the variables we apply the test as Cramer's V association.

For a significance level of 0.05, there is statistical evidence to affirm that the different variables are moderately related. In fact, it is found, that there is a direct and moderate relationship between the variables qualification and training level with gender (genderCFG), and the linear correlation coefficient r $_{(320)}$ ranges between 0.176 and 0.222 and the variable qualification is moderately relates with variable course, with correlation coefficients between 0.249 and 0.266. However, for the variable frequency of education degree (CFGMCFGS), variables "qualifications father" and mother appears to reflect other findings. However, there is no statistical evidence to affirm that the qualifications of the mother and the frequency education degree are related (VCramer $_{(320)}$ = 0.165, p -value = 0.193), so there is no influence of any qualification of the mother in the frequency of grade education, for enabling the parent to the degree of education, we can say, as previously determined dependence, these variables are associated with VCramer $_{(320)}$ = 0.199, p-value = 0.048, us it evidences in table II. It seemed to reflect about the mean difference between the qualifications of the parents. Of the 320 respondents in Barcelona, who provided information about the educational level of parents, 187 parents have equal training. The parent education is lower in 48 cases and higher in 85 cases. The number of cases in which the parent education is superior to the mother exceeds the reverse situation in almost half. The significance level of the test indicates that approximately 0% of the cases these expect to see a difference, when the null hypotheses were true.

Should reject the null hypothesis that states, there are no significant differences between the superiority of the level of education of a parent from the other. However, we intend to determine the magnitude of this difference. For this we used the Wilcoxon test, after determining the symmetry of the variable (Pereira, 2008).

The average parental skills in Barcelona to the parent when the level is higher than that of the mother is 68.7, while in the situation where the parent level is higher, the number of cases is smaller, 63.98. By bilateral significance (less than 0.05), it turns out that the difference in average attainment is high enough to reject the null hypothesis.

2.3. Study of Categories and Dimensions

Now we intend to analyze the extent to which these variables are related or not with the variables of the category "Path - Education". We applied the test of adherence Chi - Square to ensure the representativeness of the sample in each item.

In variable "retention", there are no statistical evidence to affirm that this sample is not representative, since there are no significant differences between observed and what is known of the population. Because the $\alpha^2_{(1)}$ =0,8; p-value=0,371, ensures the representativeness of the sample for retention. However, for all other variables, the p - value $<\alpha$= 0.05, which means that there is a significant difference between the mean and percentiles of the sample. It remains to investigate how these items vary.

To verify if the item "retention" is influenced by other variables (gender, nationality, nationality of parents, parents' educational and professional degree – CFGSCFGM, and "genderCFG"), we applied the test independence of Chi - Square, which revealed the existence of a relationship between variables - degree of training for Barcelona ($\alpha^2_{(1)}$ = 11.733, p-value = 0.001), "gender CFG" ($\alpha^2_{(3)}$ = 13.280, p -value = 0.04). That is to say, "retention" appears to be directly related to the degree of training and gender. The results put into discussion, that who attend CFGM – middle graduation is the young people who already were retained, and the young people who were never been retained, attending the CFGS.

So it turns out, the frequency of education in higher grades is higher in young people, who were never been retained, and there is an inverse relationship in young people who attend the middle cycles.

These two variables, and genderCFGMS and CFGMS, also appear to influence the items ("*do you think these studies will allow more easily to find a good job?*" - $\alpha^2_{(6)}$ = 14.450, p-value = 0.025. This demonstrates that the hope within education into labor market is combined with male gender and frequency of training in teaching higher grade.

In connection with item - ("*What you think to do, when you finish your studies?*", $\alpha^2_{(12)}$ = 21.024, p-value = 0.05), and the variable genderCFG, and CFGMS, suggests that the ambition to "*get a job as soon as possible*", being directly related to the training middle degree, while the training higher degree, seems to be directly linked to continuing studies. However it seems to be young people who attend the middle grade, most demanding on acceptance work.

There was a relationship between the item ("*Surely you thought what would you do if were offered you a job. Which of the following proposals, best reflects your current disposition?*" - $\alpha^2_{(6)}$ = 15.576, p-value = 0.015), and the variable genderCFG and CFGMS. However, in the higher grade, both man and female would be willing to accept any job.

We can say, with a significance level of 0.05, exits evidence to say that the acceptance of employment is related to retaining in these graduations ($\alpha^2_{(2)}$ = 6.332, p-value = 0.042).

Contrary to what would expect, are young people with retention who have more requirements before acceptance of work, therefore, young people who are willing to accept any kind of work, increases with the fact that had no retention.

With a significance level of 0.05, there is statistical evidence to affirm that the qualifications of the parents are related to items above analyses and retention - accepting employment.

With a percentage of 66.6% of young people who were retained, with greater percentage of men (among them, 176 men and 41 women and 80 men and 29 women who were never retained), is directly related to the variable nationality of the father ($\alpha^2_{(2)}$ = 14.609, p-value = 0.01), and there is a relationship with the variable - Qualification of father and mother ($\alpha^2_{(9)}$ = 25.6, p-value = 0.02, $\alpha^2_{(9)}$ = 33.008, p-value = 0.000). For these reasons, we conclude that the higher the level of parental education, the lower the observed retention of their children.

3. THEORETICAL MODEL

3.1. Linear Regression between Work and Satisfaction

In order to analyze the influence of the variable "work", we intend to estimate the value given to the work according to the evaluation that these young people make in the frequency of their course, given by "satisfaction".

We consider that the effect of "work" is explained by a constant effect, plus an effect that is proportional to the course evaluation, and a residual error (random error).

It is our expectation understands, how it is related to the valuation of work with the appreciation of the course. To do so, we proceed in a simple regression analysis between two variables - "work" (dependent) and the Item "Knowledge" of satisfaction (independent) in the course.

Before we can infer about this analysis, it is required to verify the assumptions of this regression; i) it was found a low positive and significant linear regression between the two variables, with Pearson regression = 0.112, and p-value = 0.023, the assumption of linearity is observed in the study; ii) the presupposition of errors have zero mean is verified through the analysis of residues in the sample, the assumption is verified; iii) the presupposition of homoscedasticity of errors is verified through the scatter diagrams, between residuals and standardized predicted values, standardized in the sample; iv) independence is checked by the Durbin-Watson test (DW), with the value of DW = 1.582, it is accepted that the condition is verified, then the errors are independent; v) in the case of normal distribution of errors, towards the observation and analysis of the histogram of standardized residues with overlapping of the normal curve and normal graphic PP, to check that the residues do not differ significantly from this distribution.

It can be concluded that the presuppositions are verified, therefore the regression model is valid without restrictions. However, it remains to verify the significance of the model by the F test (ANOVA). Since F = 4.007, pvalue = 0.046. As the α <0.05, the linear model is statistically significant but remains to determine whether the coefficients of the straight line regression are significant, for it, was determined t tests.

For sample analysis, the estimated model to explain and predict the appreciation of the concept of job satisfaction from the course, is given in Table III. As we can analyze, t = 13,212; pvalue <0.001, thus the model is valid statistical inferences.

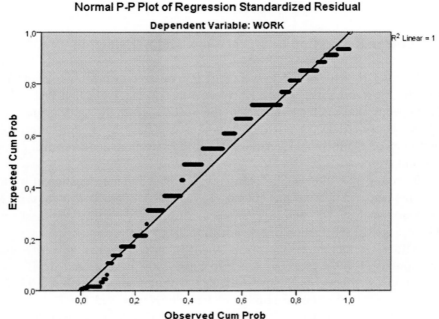

Font: own elaboration.

Figure IV. Study the relationship between the dependent variable - Work with job satisfaction.

The model has a prediction of 11% of the variation in the evaluation of the "work" explained by the assessment of "general knowledge". The prediction error is on average 2.7 with a value of intensity ratio between the estimated and observed of 0.112. The relationship although weak, it is observed that when the evaluation increases (near values to 1 or 2) decreases the value given to the job. It is demonstrated by this data, the young people who are less satisfied with the course, gives more value to the work. In other words, as the evaluation of their satisfaction to "knowledge in general" understood as "nothing important", increases the value of the work.

Taking into account the verification of the influence of satisfaction on the course with the expectation of young people about getting a job, was held the test of independence which revealed that, unlike what would be expected, there is a clear evidence to verify the satisfaction of the young people and their expectations. We conducted the Spearman test, to verify the dependency relationship between satisfaction and gender variable with training (generoCFG), as can be seen in Figure IV.

Table 3. Study of linear regression between work and evaluation

Linear regression of the course evaluation item - "general knowledge" as a predictor of the evaluation to "work"							
R^2	SE		B	SE	Beta	t	Sig.
		B0 constant	6,067	,459		13,212	,000
0,112	2,191	Evaluation of the item "general knowledge"	,331	,165	,112	2,002	,046

Font: own elaboration.

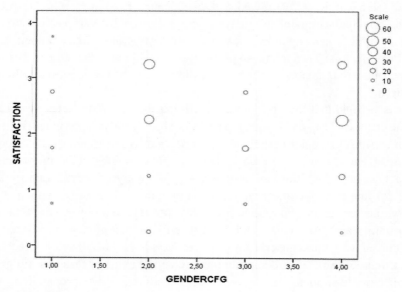

Font: own elaboration.

Figure V. Study of the relationship between job satisfaction and GENDERCFG.

For a significance level of 0.05, there are maximum statistical evidence to affirm that satisfaction is related, though negative, with generoCFG (R = - 0.120; pvalue = 0.031).

This research has shown, that the satisfaction of the course is negatively related to males and their formation, by figure V. In other words, it's these young males who give more values to work, either in the middle or upper cycle, as fewer value the course attended.

3.2. Factorial Analysis Model of Work and Educational Values

3.2.1. Analysis by Principal Components

Factor analysis includes a set of techniques that allows representing a minimum number of variables from initial variables. In this case, this analysis allows us to conclude that it is possible to explain a standard correlation, using a smaller number of variables.

This is an analysis that is intended to be confirmatory as it is used to test the initial hypothesis, that the data can be reduced to a certain size of the data and variables which distribution according to this dimension.

The factor analysis taking into account the decision criteria of Guttman-Kaiser (eigenvalues > 1.0) revealed the existence of seven factors. However, by the principal components analysis was followed by varimax rotation, a method used when applying for a simple structure, we obtained four significant factors. Through these procedures, the 35 items that enter this study grouped into four factors in the overall dimensions of the identifiers already produced.

It is verified that the first factor underlying the set of attributes associated with aspects of life, from young people is significantly represented by five variables (leisure, social participation, work, family and training), the second factor, aspects of work, are represented by eight variables (time, progression, contract, salary, conditions of progression, monotony of work, training and dynamic), the next factor, attraction to employment, is mainly explained by eight variables: salary, job type, job security, prestige, employer, environment, opportunities and promotions, and finally the fourth factor, course satisfaction, with eleven variables, general knowledge, workload, socialization, teacher / student relationship, school communities, scientific skills of teachers, program school, classification of the course, practical utility, future preparation, and context of stages. Test of sphericity Barttlett, should be rejected the null hypothesis that allows us to say there is no correlation between the initial variables. The test statistic is defined by Bartlett asymptotic distribution of $\chi2$. The KMO test obtained a value of 0.893, which indicates in the table IV, the principal component analysis can be made.

The Bartlett sphericity test gives a value of $\chi2 = 6293.688$ with 595 degrees of freedom for the sample. Viewing the table in, appears that $\chi2 > \chi2 = 0.95$, therefore reject the null hypothesis, that is, the variables are correlated. By analysis in p-value (Sig = 0.000) which is less than 0.05, it follows similarly.

Therefore, these results seem to suggest that the issue of education and employment constitutes a determining factor for life by adolescents.

Factor analysis applied to the set of items that integrate work values and educational emerges with the value of internal validation of the construct (α = 0.808), for the sample extracting four factors.

The fourth factor alone explains 54% of the total variance, with a value of internal validation of the construct (α= 0.89), representing the internal consistency of the items comprising the factor.

These explain the total variance of the values of life opinions before these young people in the sample relate to the concept of values and valuation of life before perceptions and opinions.

This factor, and according to the percentiles table, the items "free time" and "social participation", "work", "family" and "training" are perceived by 20% to 35% of the sample, as "something important" in Barcelona. The only item with equal consideration, with 103 young people (32.2%) in Barcelona, was the item "family", and the only one to be more valued in Barcelona, was the item "work" with 21.6% considering how "very important".

The third factor explains alone 47% of the total variance, with α = 0.80, attesting positive samples Barcelona. Given the percentiles table, the values of the items in relation to work, perceive themselves differently among samples. In the sample of Barcelona, the most valued item recorded was "that offers possibilities for learning" with 191 young people (59.7%). And with low percentage of recovery was the item "that is socially recognized work" with 40.6% (130 jovens in Barcelona).

Table 4. A study of the application of principal component analysis

KMO and Bartlett's Test		Barcelona
Kaiser-Meyer-Olkin Measure of Sampling Adequacy.		,893
Bartlett's Test of Sphericity	Approx. Chi-Square	6293,688
	df	595
	Sig.	,000

Font: own elaboration.

The second factor explains 32% of the total variance with a Cronbach's α= .77, which appears valid. Was named "Attraction of employment" and, according to the distribution evaluative, relating to the roles of the items, indicate the importance that certain concepts have the appreciation for a job. For example, to show the Barcelona youth classified with the most important items a "stable and secure employment", "environment and working conditions" and opportunities to make a career "as opposed to items valued less -"salary", "the kind of work that will play" and "promotional opportunities".

The first factor takes responsibility for 17% of total variance meets the classification of certain items before the satisfaction of the course that young people attending. We define this factor with the name - satisfaction, and items intended to determine the expectation of these young people in this educational pathway. However, the percentages have not varied from 40% of young people who attribute as satisfied with the course they attend. The item with the most percentage of appreciation "satisfied" was the item "general knowledge", "practical utility of education" and "socializing with friends" with 48.8% each. It was observed that there is a higher percentage of young people who are "not satisfied" with the course attending with percentages between 15.3% and 28.8%.

We understand that it is still relevant conduct a set of inferential analyzes that allows us to clarify whether membership in different courses, nationality, age and gender, implies a significant difference in the results. One of the conditions for the application of parametric tests is the normal distribution of variables, as we are working with large samples (n> 30), the application of the Central Limit Theorem may be considered to verified the presupposition (Laureano, 2011).

We can then apply the t test for two independent samples, and check if the variable gender, nationality, age and degree of professional cycle, in the case of Barcelona, interferes or not, in the valuation of the items related to the values of life, work, attraction employment and satisfaction in the course. After verifying the homogeneity of variances was assessed the value significance in t test for all items.

It may be noted that the variable gender and nationality, in Barcelona, the value of Sig> α= 0.05, so we cannot reject the null hypothesis. In fact, there is no statistical evidence for stating the average assessed valuation of the items is different in young male and young female. It is therefore concluded that the gender and nationality do not influence the value in these items studied.

However, in analyzing the degree of formation of items (CFGM / CFGS), it was found that for items "social participation", "family" relating to the life values, the value Sig = 0.000, 0.038 < α= 0.05, then rejects the null hypothesis which states that the means are equal to each degrees, we can say that the frequency of professional degrees influences the valuation given to family and social participation, curiously this is the item that is most valued by young who frequent the cycle of higher grade.

3.2.2. Analysis of Main Components by Rotation

Rotation of the principal components allows finding a new set of variable weights for each factor or component. It becomes easier to identify and interpret how each component or factor, from the weights of the variables that compose. The closer to 1 is that weight, the stronger the association between variable and factor, while a weight close to zero which, according Reis (2005), concluded that this variable does not contribute to the formation of the factor.

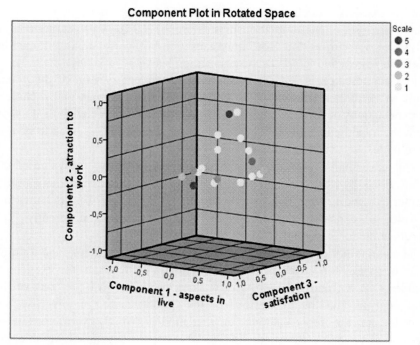

Font: own elaboration.

Figure VI. Rotation and implementation of the main components.

By this method, we can see that the sample of Barcelona, characterized three components, being significant the contribution of the variable "work", "work socially recognized" and "useful to society" in the formation of component 1, component 2 in the formation of contributes the value of the variable "salary", "type of work" and "corporate reputation", and finally to the formation of the third component, the contribution of the variable appears "scientific competence of teachers", "general knowledge" and "leisure time".

4. PATH ANALYSIS OR ANALYSIS OF PATHS OF VARIABLE "WORK"

In this part of the chapter discusses the results of the predictive study, the explanation of the analysis model of work valorization of these young people. The analysis of trajectories or path analysis is an extensive model of multiple linear regression model and aims to decompose the association between variables in a set of causal relationships (Maroco, 2007). However, a model of analysis of trajectories does not imply causation but, correlations assumed by the effects (direct and indirect), the association between variables.

All our research is based on analyzing the trajectory path of the young people in vocational education. We encounter that are distinct paths, choices and expectations of these young people in the two cities. We analyze, to what extent the hypothetical theoretical model of our research is assumed to be true and reliable.

Our case study, undertaken by different perceptions of the value of the work is done, by assuming that we can build a model of endogenous variable trajectories – work, from family and training variables. We want to show that the value of construction work, in the sample, develops differently. The theoretical model is to consider the following:

The variability of the endogenous variables mediators, family and training are, in our view, the variables whose explanation comes from the exogenous variables (X_1, X_2, and X_3), constructed from the theoretical construct of the factor analysis and the dimensions of the questionnaire. In this case, we proceeded to the representation of the models which were considered independent variables, two mediating variables and a dependent variable and the path coefficients were estimated by the standardized regression coefficients (β).

For representing the significance of the coefficients we used the respective abbreviations (*) $\leq 0{:}01$ $p < 0{:}05$ (**) $0.001 \leq p < 0.01$, (***) $p < 0.001$; opted to not put the (n) $p \geq 0{:}05$, as suggested Maroco (2010).

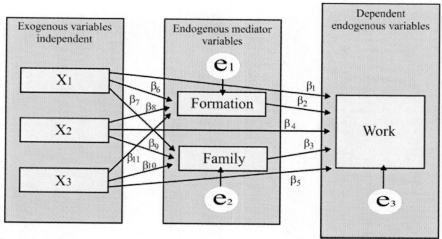

Font: own elaboration.

Figure VII. Schematic representation of the theoretical analysis.

We also determined the error, the proportion of the total variance explained by the model is not given by $E = 1 - R^2$, and the coefficient of course given by $\sqrt{1 - R^2}$. The relationship not explained is constructed by the error e_1, e_2 and e_3. The intensity of the relationship between variables is given by the path coefficients, $\beta 1$, $\beta 2$, $\beta 3$, $\beta 4$, $\beta 5$, $\beta 6$, $\beta 7$, $\beta 8$, and make up the correlation between the variables specified in the model.

The overall adjustment of the model was calculated using the coefficient of determination (R_2), considering the adjustment acceptable in social sciences to values coefficient greater than 0.5 (Maroco, 2007).

Then we proceeded to calculate the total effects through direct and indirect effects between pairs of variables. The total effects are estimates of causal association between variables. We proceeded to the following calculations, the direct effect was calculated by the standardized betas, and the indirect effect was determined by multiplying the respective standardized betas, the total effect was obtained by adding the direct effect and indirect effect. Finally, we calculated the proportion explained by causal ratio between the total effect and the correlation coefficient.

Finally, we proceeded to validate the assumptions of the regression models. Thus, it is the normality of the errors by the Kolmogorov - Smirnov, the homoscedasticity of errors through the graph of residual values versus the predicted values, independence of errors through the Durbin - Watson and multi-collinearity through factor variance inflation (VIF).

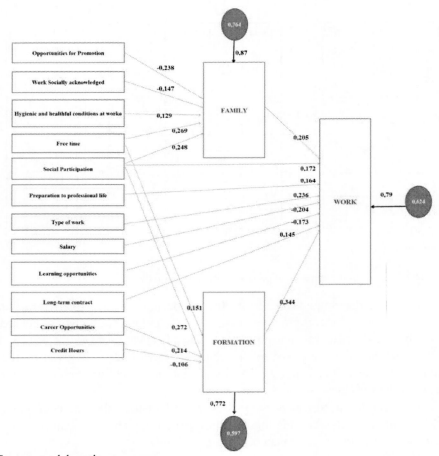

Font: own elaboration.

Figure VIII. Path analysis of work.

In the sample of Barcelona, the first model was the dependent variable, the variable family, with F = 4.471, Sig = 0.000 <α = 0.05, the linear model is adequate to explain the relationship between variables. Being the constant T statistically significant because, t = 2.198, Sig = 0.029 <α = 0.05 deducting for all variables the value of pvalue <0.005 for the slope of the line is statistically significant. With the Durbin-Watson, we can analyze the errors are not auto correlated that is, they are independent, since DW = 1.833. The coefficient R = 0.577, shows a good correlation between the intensity of variables, followed by us for analysis of the second model.

In this, we put as the dependent variable formation with F = 3.458, Sig = 0.000 <α = 0.05, the linear model is adequate to explain the relationship between variables.

Being the constant T statistically significant because, t = 3.393, Sig = 0.001 <α = 0.05 deducing for all variables the value of pvalue <0.005 for where the slope of the line is statistically significant. With the Durbin-Watson, we can analyze the errors are not auto correlated, that is, they are independent, since DW = 1.873. The coefficient R = 0.527, shows a good correlation between the intensity of variables, followed by us for analysis of the third and final model.

In this model we put in our analysis dependent endogenous variable (work), taking into account the endogenous variables mediate (family, education). With F = 6.314, Sig = 0.000 <α = 0.05, the linear model is adequate to explain the relationship between variables. The constant t = 2.934, Sig = 0.04 <α = 0.05, about the slope of the line, however, and for all variables the value of pvalue <0.005 for this to be statistically significant. With the Durbin-Watson, we can analyze the errors are not auto correlated that is, they are independent, since DW = 1.07577. The coefficient R = 0.655, shows a good correlation between intensity variables. Using the standardized regression coefficients, $\sqrt{1-R2}$ and R2-1 we can write the model trajectory analysis (figure 6). To estimate the coefficients of the trajectory of the causal model of work, it is necessary to adjust the model found the following linear regression models, structural equations:

1 FAMILY= β1Oportunidades promotion + β2social recognized + β3 healthy and hygienic conditions + β4 leisure time + β5 social participation + e1.

2 TRAINING = β6Tempo free + β7social participation + β8 Career Opportunities + β9Hour load + e2.

3 WORK = β_{10}FAMILY+ β_{11} social participation + β_{12} Preparation for professional life + β_{13} Type of work + β_{14}Salary+ β_{15} Learning opportunities $_+\beta_{16}$ Long-term contract + β_{17}Formation+ e_3.

According to this model, social participation has a direct effect on the valuation of the work of 0.172 and, an indirect effect mediated by the family, of 0.05 and still mediated by the formation with 0,093. The total effect of social participation on labor is 0.315 with 90% of the full membership of the effects work. Similarly, the salary has a direct effect, although negative, of -0.204.

Also as learning opportunities have a direct effect of 0.173, the long-term contract with a direct effect of 0.145; preparation for professional life has an effect on the work of 0,164, and the type of work with a direct effect of 0.236. The work to be socially recognized conditions and training opportunities have an indirect effect mediated by family -0.030, and -0.048 respectively. Training opportunities represent an association of 35% of the correlation between variables. The free time is a combination of correlation of 42%, which can be attributed two indirect effects, mediated by the family 0,055 and mediated formation with 0.051, with full effect 0,106. Career options, with 68% correlation between the variables and the hourly load, with 72% of the association between variables, both have an indirect effect mediated by the formation with 0.07 and 0.036 respectively.

CONCLUSION

The vocational education system focuses directly on the construction of different training itineraries, in which one can investigate strategies for capital construction. The capital acquired through this education system is not equal. The mode structure of vocational education is marked by social and economic inequalities, the crossings of different national policies are configured different itineraries. The class struggle that takes place in the two cycles is different, while the middle vocational education is directed to young people with a middle capital, legitimizing their habitus through this way. Young people who attend high graduation, have a high capital social, looking for this type of curriculum to maintain its high capital and legitimize it. The data showed that young people, who attending the middle graduation, waits for the labor market as an opportunity for life, and young people who attend the high graduation, are those who have more expectations on aspiring to further education.

The human capital theory, as we saw earlier, suggests that young people who continue their studies expect that the advantage is more intense than the cost inherent in the instruction received.

At the time that this relationship ceases to exist, the young leaves school and seeking a job, this is indeed the cornerstone of all human capital theory Schultz. As the data proved, the qualifications of the father appear to influence the frequency and choice of course. To the extent that increases the importance of titers, parents try to push their children to join secondary schools in an attempt to outline a more direct path to getting graduations or titers most prestigious.

One of the important reasons made the transition from high school is linked to parental pressure and especially young people from the working classes. This makes them reject the idea that, as Brown argues (2003), globalization has transformed the nature of the opportunities and competitiveness. As the opportunities for access to education rise, will be more difficult for young people to get follow a path of competition. Young people from lower middle classes, hopes learning a knowledge economy, exacerbated by the expansion of education itself. But the gap between those who can achieve a job with their training, and who cannot, increased. And the job market did not follow this expectation. For the opportunity depends on the occasion of each other.

The inequality between the education system and labor market opportunities produces a social misfit that affects one school generation. The generation that gets to high school, hopes that through training can achieve better jobs, but this expectation is belied by the reality offered by the labor market, as stated by Alonso (2002). This disqualification school that affects a whole generation, with titers greater than the previous generation, is the basis of collective delusion that leads this generation deceived and disillusioned to take social and cultural values different from the expected (Bourdieu, 1988).

The value of labor is associated differently in two cycles. Although these data demonstrating that the work is influenced by family and training, it takes direct effects also in social participation. However, it is these values which the youth in higher graduation most value.

Each system is a reflection of a number of systems. The education system is a system reflective of the society that embraces and integrates interrelating up. And explains at the same time, the field generated by symbolic forces. Education receives the inputs of society and to society is that the system sends its outputs. This output includes the individual formed and knowledge developed. In this empirical analysis, it was found that the young graduates of vocational training receive from society different goals, and different demands. Of course by education, we can achieve many opportunities which would not be within reach.

However, the economic capital innate creates some adjustments and remodels a force field that approximates those of you who have the capital to be reproduced. By the phenomenon of Social Darwinism, it is created opportunities for selection of the strongest economically and socially. Placing the young people, jumping degrees in degrees, in order to achieve the desired titles, like little Peter Pan's, trying to grow and grow until enter the job market and be respected.

REFERENCES

Alonso, R. (2002). *Una educación de calidad para todos. Reforma y contrarreforma educativas en la Espana actual.* Madrid: Siglo XXI.

Antunes, F. (2001). Os locais das escolas profissionais: novos papéis para o Estado e a europeização das políticas educativas. In: S. Stoer, L. Cortesão and J. A. Correia (Eds.), *Transnacionalização da educação. Da crise da educação à "educação em crise".* Porto: Edições Afrontamento.

Antunes, F. (2004a). Globalização, europeização e especificidade educativa portuguesa: A estruturação global de uma inovação nacional. (versão eletrónica). *Revista Crítica de Ciências sociais.* 70, 101-125.

Antunes, F. (2004b). Novas Instituições e processos educativos: A Educação e o modo de Regulação em Gestação. Um estudo de caso em Portugal. (versão electrónica). *Educação e Sociedade.* 25, (87), 481-511.

Baudelot, C., Establet, R. (1976). *La escuela capitalista en Francia* (J. Goded, Trans.). Madrid: Siglo XXI de Editores, S. A. (obra original publicada em).

Baudelot, C., Establet, R. (1998). *El nivel Educativo sube.* (G. Solana, Trans.). Madrid: ediciones Morata, S. L. (obra original publicada em).

Bernstein, B. (1996). *Pedagogyc Symbolic Control and Identity.* London: Taylor and Francis.

Bonal, X. (2000). *Sociologia de la educación. Una aproximación critica a las corrientes contemporáneas.* Barcelona: Paidós.

Bourdieu, P. and Passeron, J. C. (1977). *La reproducción:elementos para una teoria del sistema de enseñanza* (J. Melendres and M. Subirats, Trad.). Madrid: Editorial Popular. (Obra original publicada em1970).

Bourdieu, P. (1983). *Campo del Poder y campo intelectual* (J. Dotti, Trad.). Argentina: Gandhi, S. A. (obra original publicada em 1971).

Bourdieu, P. (1984). *Homo Academicus.* Paris: Les Editions de Minuit.

Bourdieu, P. (1986). *Distinction:a social critique of the judgement of taste.* London: Routledge.

Bourdieu, P. (1988). *La Distinction. Criterios y bases del gusto* (M. Elvira, Trad.). Madrid: Taurus. (Obra original publicada em 1986).

Bourdieu, P. (1992). *Réponses, Pour une anthroplogie réflexive.* Paris: Éditons du Seuil.

Bourdieu, P. (1993a). Effects de lieu. In: Bourdieu, P. (org). *La misère du Monde.* Paris: Éditions du Seuil.

Bourdieu, P. (1993b). L'ordre des choses. In: Bourdieu, P. (org). *La misère du Monde.* Paris: Éditions du Seuil.

Bourdieu, P. (2001). *Qué significa Hablar? Economia de los intercâmbios linguísticos.* Madrid. Akal SA.

Bourdieu, P. (2004). The forms of capital. In: Ball, S. J. (Ed.). *The Routledge Flamer Reader in Sociology Education,* (Chap. 1, 15-29). London: Routledge.

Bourdieu, P. (2010). *Capital cultural, escuela y espacio social.* (6ª ed.). (I. Jiménez, Trad.). Buenos aires, Argentina: siglo veintiumo Editores (Obra original publicada em 1997).

Brown, Phillip. (2003). The Opportunity Trap: education and employment in a global economy. *European Educational Research Journal,* 2(1), 141-179.

Dale, R. (2004, Maio/Agosto). Globalização e educação: demonstrando a existência de uma "cultura educacional mundial comum" ou localizando uma "agenda globalmente estruturada para a educação"? (versão eletronica), *Educação e Sociedade,* 25(87), 423 – 460.

Enguita, M. (1985b). *Trabalho, escuela e ideología.* Mardrid: Akal.

Garcia, R. (2008). Habitus y clase social en Bourdieu: una aplicación empírica en el campo de los deportes de combate. *Papers,* 89, 103-125.

Hill, M. M. and Hill, A. (2002). *Investigação por questionário.* Lisboa: Edições Sílabo.

Hinojal, I. (1980). *Educacion Y Sociedad. Las sociologías de la educacio.* Madrid: CIS.

Horcajo, J. (1979). *La Cultura Reproduccion O Campo.* Madrid: Rumagraf, S. A.

Horcajo, J. (1991). *Escuela, sistema y sociedade Invatación a la sociologia de la Educación.* Madrid: Prodhufi, SA.

Iregui, G. (2002). *Pierre Bourdieu, conceptos básicos y construcción socioeducativa.* Colombia: Panamerica formas e impressos SA.

Jover, D. (2006). *Praxis de la esperanza. Educación, empleo y economia social.* Barcelona: Romanyà/Valls.

Laureano, Raul M. S. (2011). *Testes de Hipóteses.* Lisboa: Edições Silabo.

Maroco, João. (2007). *Análise Estatística.* Lisboa: Edições Silabo.

Mir, R. (1990). *Sociologia de la educación. Guia Didactica y Textos Fundamentales.* Madrid: Hispagraphis, SA.

Navas, A., Martinez, I., Gómez, L. (2004). Mercado y educación:seduciones y decepciones In: *Identidades y formación para el trabajo* (pp. 67-104). Genebra: Cinterfor.

Perales, I. (2008). *Génesis de la Teoria social de Pierre Bourdieu.* Madrid: Graficas Arias Montano.

Pestana, M. H. and Gageiro, J. N. (2009). *Análise de dados em Ciências Sociais* (5.ª Edição). Lisboa: Edições Sílabo.

Reis, E. (2001). *Estatística Multivariada aplicada*. Lisboa: Edições Silabo.

Sierra, J. F. (2001). La orientación profesional en la enseñanza obligatoria: algunas contradicciones educativas. In: L. Vega (coord.). *Trabajo, Educacion y Cultura. Un enfoque interdisciplinar*. pp. 197-210. Madrid: Lavel SA.

Silva, C. (2012a). The Cycles of Vocational Training in the region of Barcelona. In: *Procedia - Social and Behavioral Sciences*, 69, 1931 – 1937.

Silva, C. (2012b). Capital Económico e Capital Cultural. Ciclos Formativos Profissionais em Barcelona. In: XVI Conferencia de Sociología de la Educación. *La educación en la sociedad global e informacional*. 12 e 13 Jul. 2012. Oviedo.

Teodoro, A. (2008). Novos modos de regulação transnacional de políticas educativas. Evidências e possibilidades. In: A. Teodoro. *Tempos e andamentos nas políticas de educação. Estudos ibero-americanos*, (19-38). Brasilia: Liber Livro Editora.

In: Labor Markets   ISBN: 978-1-62948-662-8
Editor: William E. Grossman   © 2014 Nova Science Publishers, Inc.

Chapter 2

A LINGERING DECLINE OR A STABLE FUTURE? THE CASE FOR INVESTING IN RURAL TOURISM[*]

Gordon B. Cooke[1†], Jennifer K. Burns[2] and Kyle W. J. Vardy[2]

[1]Associate Professor, Industrial Relations,
Memorial University of Newfoundland, Canada
[2]Graduate, Master of Employment Relations,
Memorial University of Newfoundland, Canada

ABSTRACT

Partially due to the effects of globalization, rural communities within industrialized nations have had to endure economic restructuring as manufacturing and traditional industries such as small-scale fishing or farming have been replaced by service industry-based economies. We would argue that it is important to differentiate between near-rural (or suburban) communities and more remote, truly 'rural' communities. In the latter, where individuals cannot commute for daily work to an urban center, populations tend to be declining, at least on a relative basis. For

[*] This research was supported by a grant from the Social Sciences and Humanities Research Council of Canada (SSHRC) (#864-2007-0090), as well as by a SSHRC/VP Grant from Memorial University of Newfoundland.
[†] Corresponding author: gcooke@mun.ca.

these rural communities to remain vibrant, many will need to embrace new industries as a means of maintaining employment and economic activity. Using two examples from the Canadian province of Newfoundland and Labrador, we advocate for the investment of public funds to try to sustain rural communities by boosting tourism visitors, and hence, revenues and employment. Industrialized nations like Canada have seen a growing 'casualization' of jobs in the labor market, and this trend is often accentuated in rural communities where unemployment tends to be higher, and seasonal employment is prevalent. Tourism, and certainly rural tourism, is also very likely to be a seasonal exercise, and as such, it can be argued that it generates only poor quality jobs. We view this from a different angle. Developing a seasonal tourism industry in a rural area can be a way to provide a level of economic sustainability, but without undermining local historical, social, and cultural norms and activities. In fact, if public funds are used to improve and expand rural infrastructure and the number of events and activities, then visitors and local citizens both benefit, especially when those events and activities revive or maintain local traditions. Moreover, the seasonal and/or part-time jobs created by tourism potentially fit the needs of older rural individuals, while also providing opportunities for local entrepreneurs once public funds have created sufficient tourist activity. We view this approach as being far more desirable than doing nothing while rural communities try to cope with economic restructuring and declining populations. That said, developing a tourism industry requires ongoing, significant capital investments to create a critical mass of attractions and events, and even then, someone, or some group, within the community needs to champion the cause. While developing tourism is expensive and time-consuming and the prospects for success are far from guaranteed, we ask: If not tourism, then what policy alternatives offer better prospects?

INTRODUCTION

The reality of labor markets in Canada and elsewhere in much of the developed world is polarized working conditions. While some 'lucky' workers hold high-paying, secure jobs with social status, pleasant working conditions, and access to a range of company-provided benefits, many others are only able to access lower quality jobs in terms of things like pay, benefits, job security, status, and other working conditions (Betcherman and Lowe, 1997; Zeytinoglu, 1999). Factors affecting the quality of employment that one can access include the acquisition of the valued skills and work experiences sought by employers. Thus, at first blush, it would appear that people can determine the level of luck that they have by the effort they expend. We believe, however, that personal and family circumstances are factors that are difficult for any individual to change. Furthermore, workers are subject to geographic luck in addition to effort, since the opportunities to acquire skills, education, and work experience can be much lower for those in rural locations relative to those in more urbanized centers. While the reality of rural economic challenges and an urban-rural employment (and income) gap has been documented in academic and other literature, the solutions seemingly have received less attention, presumably because there are no 'quick fixes'. The public policy conundrum is whether or not governments have a role to address the challenges facing rural workers, and if so, the manner in which to intervene. We believe that there has been insufficient or ineffective public policy intervention, and this has contributed to, or at least not prevented, rural communities from enduring weak economic conditions, a lack of economic diversification, aging and declining populations, and the prospect of declining services and infrastructure in the future. Part of the problem is that multiple levels of governments have struggled to avoid or eliminate deficits as they try to manage in today's global economy. In turn, spending of public funds on infrastructure has been constrained or delayed. Yet, now is the time for action.

The purpose of this paper is to present the role that tourism could and should play in the economies of rural communities enduring employment challenges. Tourism is the focus because it has been touted by many people- in government, in rural areas, and in business- as a possible panacea for struggling communities (e.g. Constantin and Mitrut, 2009; Government of NL, 2009; Government of PEI, 2010; Cooke, Burns, and McManamon, 2013; Irshad, 2010). In our view, having tourism sustain rural communities is easy to dream about, but difficult to achieve in practice. On the other hand, investing in the tourism industry is an attractive approach given the policy alternatives available to decision-makers. To some extent, we base our argument on a series of 35 semi-structured interviews with participants directly or indirectly involved in operating a business, tourism, and/or community development. These interviews were conducted primarily in Newfoundland, Ireland, and Shetland between September 2010 and January 2013. We also rely on insights from an additional 135 interview participants in similar jurisdictions during 2009 and 2010, a small number of tourist surveys gathered as a part of a pilot study during 2012 and 2013, and previous studies that we have published.

Rather than a review of existing literature or a summary of our empirical findings, this chapter contains our argument for the investment of public dollars into the tourism industry in rural communities who require economic help. We will be using two examples from the Canadian province of

Newfoundland and Labrador: Trinity Bight and Fogo Island. Within each of these, which are really groupings of small rural villages, there are community movements to develop and expand their local economies via tourism. While we will be discussing Canadian examples, we also believe that our analyses will be of interest to those concerned about the sustainability of rural communities elsewhere. After providing some background information on today's economic and employment realities, we then turn to the policy options pertaining to rural communities. Subsequently, we make our case for a sustained investment of public funds into rural tourism, and also present sample views from participants in and around Fogo Island and Trinity Bight, followed by concluding thoughts.

THE TRUE 'NEW ECONOMY', EMPLOYMENT GAPS, AND RURAL REALITIES

There are seemingly mixed messages about the state of employment in North America. There are labor shortages, but only for those in rare occupations with specialized skills, or in pocketed areas with tight labor markets. Other than these exceptions, the opposite has occurred, namely a 'casualization' of the world of work (e.g. Betcherman and Lowe, 1997). By casualization, we mean the prevalence of jobs with other than open-ended, full-time, full-year hours. These include part-time, temporary/seasonal, fixed-term, and on-call jobs. Employers are the ones primarily responsible for implementing conditions of work (Kochan, Katz, and McKersie, 1986), and if there is a need for only part of a full-time, full-year worker, and if there are sufficiently attractive workers available who are willing to accept those conditions, then that is likely the way that work will be structured (see Zeytinoglu, Cooke, and Mann, 2009; Verma and Chaykowski, 1999). Thus, the unfortunate reality that working conditions in Canada and elsewhere have become highly polarized. The 'lucky' ones are able to acquire good quality employment in terms of full-time status (or part-time if they prefer it), access to company-provided benefits, control over work hours and location, and job security. However, the rest are less lucky, and are either enduring, or at risk of enduring, only jobs with low pay, few benefits, uncertain or unattractive hours, casual employment status, and little upward mobility. While this trend has been documented for many years (e.g. Betcherman and Lowe, 1997; Cooke, 2007; Zeytinoglu, 1999), there is a growing sense that these labor market divisions are more entrenched than ever. There have, of course, always been casual and part-time jobs, certainly from the early days of the industrial revolution, and earlier. Relative to the post-WWII era of high employment and growing prosperity, North America has been confronted since the 1970s by energy shocks, economic restructuring, an aging society, deficit and debt challenges, and the pressure to compete in a global market against emerging economies with cheap labor. In response to these pressures, employers are more inclined- and able- to impose conditions of work that suit operational needs rather than employee wants (see, for example, Cooke et al., 2008; Verma and Chaykowski, 1999; Chaykowski and Gunderson, 2001; Betcherman and Lowe, 1997).

On the whole, the more skills and education that a person has, the more likely they can be among the lucky ones able to demand and receive good quality employment (e.g. Betcherman and Lowe, 1997; Cooke, 2007). The corollary, however, is that those with less power in the labor market are more likely to be stuck in poor quality employment. Moreover, skills and education are only some of the factors accounting for low power, with others being things like personal characteristics such as gender, age, ethnicity, or family circumstances (Saunders, 2003; Vallée, 2005). Power is the key, though. Thus, in situations in which workers have low power relative to employers, poor conditions of work are likely to be the result. While urban workers are subject to economic cycles, and the increasing importance of holding valued skills, the situation is even more acute for rural workers. Thus, while one's power is affected by personal choices, it is also subject to uncontrollable factors including geographic location. Unfortunately, there are numerous ways in which 'rural' communities or 'rurality' is defined. Sometimes rural is defined using population size only, with communities defined as either urban or rural on the basis of an arbitrary cut-off point, and without regard to physical location. Since an exploration of the various ways of defining 'rural' is far beyond the scope of this chapter, we simply indicate that we view communities as fitting into one of three general categories: urban, suburban/near rural, and truly rural. By the latter, we mean small communities with at least some degree of remoteness. That is, one where there are few businesses, and where it is impractical to commute on a daily basis to an urban center, for work or otherwise. The more 'rural' a community is, the more likely it is that the community is struggling to maintain population and its economic base (Vera-Toscana, Phimister, and Weersink, 2004).

While the definition of 'rural' is elusive, the economic realities of rural living are less so. According to measures such as income levels, access to full-time, full-year work, or job stability, on average, employment conditions are poorer in rural areas in Canada (see Vera-Toscana, Phimister, and Weersink, 2004; Cooke, Donaghey, and Zeytinoglu, 2013). Key obstacles to rural economic vibrancy include a lack of economic diversification, varying degrees of isolation from customers, clients, businesses and services; and transportation limitations (Alasia, 2010; Cooke and Mann, 2011; Vera-Toscana, Phimister, and Weersink, 2004). To be blunt, rural individuals are subject to geographic bad luck since the opportunities to acquire skills, education, and work experience are lower, on average, relative to their urban counterparts. This rural-urban divide, while real and important, is only the initial problem. The effect of those rural issues is divergent choices for younger versus older generations. The general pattern that we have observed is that the older individuals who value a rural lifestyle are likely to make the best of whatever employment is locally available, while older individuals prioritizing financial wants over lifestyles are candidates for out-migration. We have found that the vast majority of older rural individuals fit into the former category, and will only reluctantly out-migrate if minimal financial requirements cannot be met within their current community (Cooke, Donaghey, and Zeytinoglu, 2013).

The situation is starker for young rural people, since- as described above-employment prospects, and locally available post-secondary institutions can be limited. Consequently, young people often have difficulty acquiring the skills, education and work experience to break into good quality employment, or even a path towards it. Yet, this is occurring at a time when the need for skills beyond high school has become increasingly apparent. In fact, we have found that many of these individuals have thought deeply about accepting a 'hometown discount' in order to remain in the communities where they feel most comfortable. That is, these individuals have decided how much better pay, benefits, promotion opportunities or job security would need to be elsewhere *before* they will leave their hometown communities. In a comparable study of young nursing graduates from Newfoundland and Labrador, remaining close to family, friends and 'home' was a recurring theme among 70% of participants (Burns, 2012). However, as noted earlier, individuals with few skills and little work experience will likely have very little power in the labour market; and this at a career stage when those workers cannot afford to be stuck in a dead-end job for long. Older workers, especially if owning a (mortgage-free) house, might be able to 'gear down' and manage on casual work, but a young adult needs a path to steady work, the opportunity to begin to create a retirement nest egg, and a chance for advancement. As a result, young people are more likely to out-migrate, reluctantly or otherwise, for better opportunities elsewhere (Bernard, Finnie, and St-Jean, 2008). Such out-migration has occurred in Atlantic Canada for decades because a lack of labour demand by traditional employers produced a need for more than short-term income replacement among workers (Freshwater, 2008). In Canada, perhaps the most well-known case of "brain drain" – or the loss of skilled workers – is that of Newfoundland and Labrador where upwards of 30, 000 of the province's population now live and work in the Oil sands in Northwestern Canada to pursue better employment. This all contributes to the relative aging and declining populations in rural communities, especially those distant from urban centers. As a result, rural unemployment rates tend to be higher, bouts of unemployment last longer, and labour force participation is lower (CCL, 2006), and relative income levels have slipped (OECD, 2006).

Given these circumstances, one might feel that governments have an obligation to try to improve the plight of rural individuals, when and where conditions are tangibly poorer, and options more limited, than in urban centers. But, another reality is that the governments in Canada and the US- like many in the industrialized world- continue to struggle to manage their deficit and debt levels. Therefore, any policy responses for rural communities need to be financially prudent if involving investment of public funds.

THE ALTERNATIVES

Before summarizing the policy alternatives, we reiterate some earlier points of discussion. On the whole, older rural individuals tend to be willing and able to tolerate casual employment, as long as it provides a minimum threshold of income and security (to allow them to stay in their preferred community). There is also a group of emigrants, currently living away, who could be enticed to return if sufficiently attractive opportunities materialize. In fact, many of these rural emigrants are hoping for a change in employment conditions so that they can return. Young individuals, however, fall into one of two main camps after leaving high school. Either they are willing to take any available local employment as a stop-gap measure (to see if better opportunities emerge, or to decide where to out-migrate for work or education), or they have decided to leave immediately for better opportunities elsewhere (Cooke, 2012). There are also a number of young individuals keen to stay near their rural roots, but who are ambitious, and are acquiring more skills and qualifications at nearby post-secondary institutions. Some of these are in technical fields, hospitality, tourism, and business programs. They would be more than willing to remain in their current location, but only if a path to good employment materializes.

The challenge is to balance financial feasibility at a time of budget constraints, while recognizing that there are citizens with different needs and expectations within rural communities who need governments to act. In terms of addressing rural economic conditions, the policy choices available to governments fall into the five main alternatives:

1. *Do nothing.* This default option would result in the slow and continued decline of many rural communities.
2. *Resettlement.* Acting to speed up the relocation/migration of rural people to larger communities. While sounding far-fetched, there actually are examples where this approach has explicitly or implicitly been taken.
3. *Handouts.* Implementing policies to allow rural/remote people to live comfortably, independent of local employment options. This would involve some form of social (i.e. welfare) payments not tied to employment.
4. *Relocation.* Facilitating the movement of rural people to other communities to seek temporary or ongoing employment opportunities. This would seek to reduce structural unemployment by incentivizing unemployed individuals to out-migrate from areas of high unemployment to areas with labour shortages.
5. *Investment.* Strengthening rural economies so that there are better employment opportunities for local citizens. This would involve either direct investment of public funds into areas of high unemployment, or policy changes to encourage the investment of private funds.

First, it is necessary to state unequivocally that these five options are not equally attractive to us, nor would they be to members of rural communities. Nonetheless, before advocating investment in tourism, alternatives deserve to be considered. It seems to us that Option 2 (Resettlement), which indeed means involuntary relocation, is highly controversial and political, and is seen by critics (and many neutrals) as being inappropriate, callous, and/or presumptuous to force people to relocate from their preferred location. This approach has been used previously, and is still the cause of controversy many decades later. Since it restricts people from living where they prefer, Option 2 is a non-starter for us. Option 3 (Handouts) is impractical given today's economic realities and the fiscal situation of the Canadian and Newfoundland governments. It would involve increasing the ease by which rural individuals could receive income supports independent of their employment status, and would need to involve more generous payouts than are currently provided (while admitting that the level of current 'generosity' is also highly debated). It also wouldn't address the psychological aspect since people would miss the feeling of accomplishment from earning what they receive. For both reasons, we view Option 3 as unworkable. Options 1 (Do nothing) and 4 (Relocation) are possibilities because they would be less contentious, but would still seem to have negative implications. Option 1 would result in the continued slow decline of population- triggered by out-migration of mostly younger people- which would exacerbate the provision of government services land loss of customer bases for local businesses. Option 4 would result in a better match of workers to jobs at a macro level, but not all people are mobile, and those remaining in the shrinking and struggling areas would have to endure deteriorating services. Thus, Options 1 and 4 would not address the decline of rural communities. In contrast, the biggest negative associated with Option 5 (Investment) is that there can be a natural reluctance - on the part of policy makers - for public funds to be invested in a manner where the benefits to the 'receiving' community emerge over time, and where the precise financial returns are difficult to quantify. That reluctance is understandable, since critics love to mock 'wasteful' government spending. Nevertheless, we believe that while the rate of return on investment in rural infrastructure or direct job creation can be low or difficult to quantify, the broader social benefits that accrue are real and important. The issue comes down to whether or not governments are willing and able to try to sustain, if not revitalize, rural communities that are in need. If the answer is yes, then Option 5 (Investment) is the preferred approach. If not, then communities needing action are going to watch governments miss an opportunity to help.

PARTICIPANTS' VIEWS FROM NEWFOUNDLAND EXAMPLES: FOGO ISLAND AND TRINITY BIGHT

Semi-structured interviews have been conducted with 35 individuals involved, directly or indirectly, in business, tourism, and/or community development in rural Newfoundland, Ireland, and Shetland between September 2010 and January 2013. These interviews were a follow-up to a larger study involving 135 participants in those same jurisdictions between February 2009 and September 2010. Within these three jurisdictions, communities were selected to have comparable levels of remoteness and community size. The rationale was this could facilitate analysis of the individual, government, and community responses to rural economic conditions. In this chapter, sample comments from selected participants are shown, to provide a sense of the views of local citizens to tourism, economic conditions, government policies, and related community issues[1].

Since our position about the need to invest in tourism primarily emerged from studying rural Newfoundland, two community examples from within this Canadian province are presented. Newfoundland is the island portion of Canada's most easterly province, and is a large land mass containing only slightly more than half a million residents within its North Atlantic location. As such, visitors from more populated American or international locations tend to view the whole province as being somewhat remote and rural. Fogo Island is a grouping of several small communities on an island 20 miles (25 kilometers) long, accessible via 45 minute ferry ride from a port that is four hours away from the capital city of St. John's, and one hour away from the nearest town. While it has a fascinating history, unusual topography, and charming villages and people, it is a long way from major airports and the capital region, has a population of only slightly more than 2,000 people in total, and rather limited shopping and services, notwithstanding the recent initiatives of the Shorefast Foundation. Shorefast is primarily funded by Ms. Zita Cobb, a wealthy benefactor who has returned to her hometown with a dream to revitalize the local economy of the area by accentuating its art, culture, and history.

It now consists of several full-time and part-time workers and advisors, all equally enthusiastic about its mandate. In addition to Ms. Cobb's funds, Shorefast is also supported by funds from the federal and provincial government (see Shorefast Foundation (2013) for more details), and has initiated a number of community events for locals and visitors, has encouraged related micro business start-ups, and has recently opened a small, high-end 'inn' (i.e. boutique hotel) to generate employment and tourist revenues without cannibalizing existing businesses. Until Shorefast began its development projects around five years ago, tourism in the area was very small scale and was seasonal. To be fair, it still is, although there are numerous signs of new activity.

---

[1] Additional methodological details are available from the first author, upon request.

Table 1. Selected Comments from Trinity Bight and area

Participant info	Location and date	Comment(s)
Female and male; tourism business operators, ages: 60+	An area close to, and in competition with, Trinity Bight; Sept 2011	"The tourist season is way too short to make a good living. It really is only strong for six weeks from mid-July to the end of August." "Too many locals don't want tourists. They are not entrepreneurial. It's very hard to run a business locally. The government and locals aren't actively trying to grow tourism."
Male, tourism operator; age: 60+	Trinity Bight; June, 2011	"You have to love being in this business to survive. It really doesn't make much money at all. We have to watch our costs closely and do as much work ourselves as possible." "The Rising Tide Theatre is key for tourism in this area. When they extended their fall season, that extended the tourist season for everyone around here".
		'The Trinity Historical Society is doing such good work to separate Trinity Bight from other areas of province with activities, architecture, museums. That's something different and nice to do".
Male, in tourism and community development; age: 20s	Trinity Bight; Sept 2010	"One problem is that local government services are slowly leaving the peninsula and being moved [to a more central urban center]. This is in addition to the commercial activity that is shifting there too." "There is a chicken and egg issue. Small towns cannot afford to hire an economic development officer. On the other hand, the lack of economic development on the commercial/industrial side prevents [us] from growing revenues to the able to hire one." We have been trying for years to extend the tourism seasons into September and October, but it is a tough sell. After Labour day, most of the tourists to this area are from the [capital region]. However, those people won't return to the Rising Tide theater probably, since they repeat the plays from the spring/summer". "There is a catch-22 situation. The restaurant and pub don't stay open because the B&Bs have fewer customers. However, the B&Bs might have fewer customers when the theater has closed for the season and the restaurants are closed. Everyone knows the problems but it's hard to get one or two business owners to take a chance, so others can benefit"

Trinity Bight is less remote, but is nonetheless about a three hour drive from the St. John's, also consists of several small communities, and has a total population of roughly 2,000 people. It has several museums within historical buildings that have been refurbished by the Trinity Historical Society (THS), as well as the Rising Tide Theatre which features numerous plays and performances throughout the summer and into the fall. It is well known as a tourist destination, has a stunning location, and has had a tourism industry for at least a couple decades. There are several accommodations providers in the area, and several other tourism/hospitality operations. On the other hand, tourism in the area is still highly seasonal, and the surrounding area has been suffering from declining population, closures in the fishery, and infrastructure issues compounded by damage from a recent hurricane. Each year, substantial grants from the federal and provincial governments are used to operate the set of museums and the theatre's schedule of performances. Both of these examples involve community-level initiatives to boost tourism, and in both locations, local citizens have placed significant emphasis on preservation of local culture and history. While Trinity Bight does not enjoy the financial support of a wealthy benefactor, it does have significant grassroots community involvement, and is led by passionate town officials and volunteers. In the following two tables, selected comments are provided to show some of the representative tourism-related views within these communities.

Simultaneously, there were strong feelings that while visitors are welcome, rural citizens live in these locations for a reason. Many would like a longer tourist season, but NOT a year-round season. Many rural citizens value peace and tranquility, and so it is possible, or even likely, that a partial-year tourist season would be viewed as more desirable than a full-year tourist season. Also, most are very concerned about providing authentic experiences to visitors, rather than being 'kitschy'. This is actually a benefit, because it doesn't require a rural community to have to have a plan to entice tourists all year. Instead, the challenge is to grow a tourist industry to a sufficient level to create seasonal jobs each year, with enough security that a person can count on the annual income.

On Fogo Island, there are a growing number of tourists coming to visit the trails and festivals, but especially to see the crafts, art studios, and other investments initiated by the Shorefast Foundation. In turn, new B&Bs and rental cottages have opened, although more visitors are needed to be able to support new restaurants, pubs, and cafes.

Table 2. Selected Comments from Fogo Island and area

Participant info	Location and date	Comment(s)
Male, employed in tourism and related industries; age: 50s	Fogo Island; Sept 2011	"It's hard to make a living at fishing or agriculture here. The Shorefast stuff won't last forever, unless the jobs that are created are sustainable. They cannot afford to subsidize forever".
Participant info	Location and date	Comment(s)
Female; employed outside of the tourism industry; age: 50s	Fogo Island; Sept 2011	"I don't think that tourism will be the savior of Fogo Island, but it is one more thing to help us diversify [our economy]". "Local governance has been an obstacle to development. We need to cooperate between communities better." "We could use an interpretative center for tourists, and public washrooms. We don't have any!"
Male, retired from job not related to tourism; age: 60+	Fogo Island; Sept 2011	"The point is not to knock Fogo Island. Rather, the reasons why people should make the extra effort to come here is unclear to me."
Male, employed in tourism and related industries; age: 30s	Fogo Island; June 2012	"Tourists are going to visit Twillingate before or after coming here. We need to work together. There is a shortage of expertise in tourism. There are also lots of mom and pop operations and so coordination is a big problem.""We can't be kitschy- we need to be authentic." "Shorefast has 'put wind in our sails'. More people are already coming here and there is more pride and confidence". "We need to do something to prevent more out-migration. Tourism is still small-scale, but growing".
Female and male; tourism business operators, ages: 60+	Fogo Island; Sept 2011	"We don't need to make money with our business. It would be nice, but we don't have the pressure that some others face. We are doing as more of a hobby. It's something that we love".
Female; employed in tourism; age: 60+	Fogo Island; Aug 2012	"There needs etter coordination between the communities and between things like the museums. Tourists don't know what to do around here. We need them [to have more things to do] to stay 2 or 3 days longer."
Female; employed in tourism; age: 50s	Fogo Island; June 2012	"People like showing off the area to visitors. People like to welcome guests, but then also relax and take a breath and enjoy when the tourist season is over". "Some of the workers at Shorefast probably love the money, but some must [still] be unsure about the future".
		"There are lots of [rural] workers who just want to get their weeks in [i.e. to qualify for employment benefits] but others will work more if given the chance".

Tourists and locals are also concerned about the reliability, comfort and accessibility of the ferry service. This essentially will act as a bottleneck to tourism growth until more public funds improve convenience for tourists (which will benefit locals as well). In and around Trinity Bight, a common view was that tourism is well established, and that there are lots of facilities (e.g. signage, accommodations, parking, live theater, museums, and boat tours) for visitors. We would agree, but also note that the tourist season essentially operates while the publicly subsidized theater is operating. As such, the tourism industry is not yet self-sustaining. Nonetheless, several private tourism businesses operate in the area. Thus, this area needs publicly funded events to stretch the tourist into the spring or fall period, and to deepen the intensity of the tourist season, so that existing business owners require -and can afford- to hire more local seasonal workers. The irony is that a minority of people in and around Fogo Island indicated that they do not want to have a tourist industry as large as the one in Trinity Bight. We hope that a middle ground can be reached where a tourism industry can be large enough to yield economic benefits for a rural community or region, but not so large that current lifestyles, norms, and traditions are tangibly harmed. Currently, the situation in both of our community examples is that it would be better if there were more facilities and attractions for tourists, which also means more ways for the communities to generate revenues from those visitors.

THE CASE FOR INVESTING IN TOURISM

After reviewing the above policy alternatives- several of which were highly undesirable, the choice appears to be to do nothing, or to invest in rural communities. That is a political choice, and one that needs to be made according to local resources, needs, and politics. We would say, though, that it would be a lost opportunity to do nothing, since the result would likely be a continued decline in the population and economies of remote, rural areas. If the choice is made to invest in rural communities, then we believe that tourism could be the answer, for two main reasons: i) feeling of accomplishment and social benefits for locals including increased community spirit, and ii) fit with employment needs.

Feeling of Accomplishment and Social Benefits

While rural individuals often want governments to implement more generous policies to boost rural economies, our past research (i.e. Cooke, Donaghey, and Zeytinoglu, 2013) indicates that these rural citizens generally want an opportunity to do meaningful work. Most especially, these individuals want work with social value that can help their community, rather than receive a mere handout. We believe that tourism is a good fit because it can be used to complement existing activity. A community with fishing heritage can educate and entertain visitors with glimpses of its past, even if current activity has declined. Moreover, if there still is local commercial activity, then visitors are an obvious potential market for harvesters and local restaurateurs to target. Similarly, a community with a tradition of farming might try to develop agriculturally based festivals and 'working farm vacations' as a way to blend old traditions with newer visitor-enticing activities. Alternatively, a community with natural beauty or space needs to accentuate those possible strengths in a way that will entice visitors to come, while also providing an added benefit for locals. Plus, as noted by the above, rural people tend to be keen to show off the benefits of their local sights and sounds to interested visitors. Thus, tourism offers the potential of win-win outcomes if the events or attractions that are developed build upon, and provide a way to retain, local traditions, customs, and lifestyles (Irshad, 2010).

While building a marketing plan is beyond the scope of this chapter, communities need to ponder the options within tourism. One option is to focus on cultural tourism, which means accentuating museums, landscapes, and communities, as well as music, folklore and traditions (Timothy, 2011). Thus, cultural tourism, unlike other ways to attract visitors, focuses on the arts, heritage and history of a place (Raj, 2003). Since many rural areas tend to have a distinct culture and way of life, at least compared to urban norms, that can lend itself to the development of cultural tourism activities and events (Cooke, Burns, and McManamon, 2013). This type of tourism employment can be very rewarding for an individual who has a great sense of attachment or connection to a particular location and who enjoys sharing their experiences and hometown with others. As a result, rural tourism initiatives not only enhance and revitalize community pride, but can also aid in the preservation of rural culture and heritage (Irshad, 2010). A different option is to build rural tourism by accentuating the available space. While some might find it kitschy, if land values are lower, then tourism facilities that take space - like amusement centers, golf courses or campgrounds- might be viable where land and labour is cheaper and more readily available. We do not necessarily advocate this type of tourism. Rather, our point is that any type of tourism in rural areas- if implemented strategically- offers potential benefits for visitors and locals alike, since it means more activities, more events, more facilities, more options, and more employment than before. Irshad (2010) goes further, and notes how the revenues from tourism can assist rural communities in the retention of services such as retailing, transport, hospitality, and medical care that are at risk of being lost if populations continue to decline. This is important, since communities are not sustainable in the long term unless there are jobs and services that can be maintained (see McElwee and Whittam, 2012).

Fit with Employment Needs

Although it might seem counterintuitive, past research suggests that many rural individuals, especially older ones, would be quite satisfied to be able to work in an industry if they could rely on at least a few months of work annually without having to relocate, since it offers a chance to remain in their chosen community (see Cooke, Donaghey, and Zeytinoglu, 2013). It is true that many tourism jobs pay at or near the local minimum wage and usually offer few employer-provided benefits (e.g. Elkin and Roberts, 1994). However, even the casual, part-time, or temporary forms of work that a short tourist season brings could allow a person in a rural community to avoid relocation, and become more reliant on their own income generation as opposed to direct reliance on income supports. Since tourism is a field with low barriers to entry - that is, many of the jobs will be entry-level jobs - special credentials or education will not be required. While some training will be required, it will be of a nature that can be provided locally, or even on-the-job. Paradoxically, this is beneficial because this means that unemployed, difficult-to-employ, persons changing industries, and adults of all ages will be able to access these jobs. Thus, it can allow rural individuals who hold casual or seasonal work to augment their incomes by working in tourism concurrently, or during off periods (Lagravinese, 2012).

A key goal of public investment in rural tourism is job creation. Both the development and maintenance of infrastructure, and the ongoing servicing of the tourist population would create jobs in rural locales that otherwise would see little opportunity. The Newfoundland and Labrador tourism industry supported over 10,000 jobs for the province's people in 2010 (Government of

NL, n.d.), among a total population of only 520,000. Since tourism in Newfoundland is still in a growth phase, it is logical to think that more job creation in the tourism industry (including infrastructure development) would lead to better options for native Newfoundlanders and Labradorians. This type of job creation will generate individual income that can ease the burden of government when it comes to social assistance for unemployed individuals. Additionally, we feel that tourism is a catalyst for entrepreneurial spirit. As we have identified in this paper, while many citizens of rural communities may leave for employment opportunities, there are more who are unwilling or unable to leave their hometowns. An influx of tourist interest in a small community means that there is a niche to be filled in many small towns. Whether providing food, shelter, clothing, souvenirs or activities for tourists, there are countless rural communities who have seen struggling homemakers and fisher persons become bed and breakfast owners and boat tour guides. The benefit to government is twofold. One, there is a desired tourist service available as a result of the new enterprise (food, shelter or otherwise) which likely came at little cost to government in terms of infrastructure investment; and two, the self-employed individual may be able to provide for themselves instead of having to rely on government assistance or having to relocate. As such, there are also opportunities for local entrepreneurs, once governments have built the infrastructure and attracted a base of guests. This might also attract some of the more highly educated, ambitious younger people, who would be out-migration risks, to consider starting their own business, or finding a management-track position within a growing business (see Irshad, 2010; Cooke, Burns, and McManamon, 2013). Currently the bulk of tourism operations within the province are of a 'mom and pop' nature, and many of the operators run their business as more of a hobby or service to the area rather than as a primary income generator. Although people have a tendency to be financially conservative, we attribute the prevalence of small-scale businesses to the size of the current tourism industry. A current operator had better have motivations other than money making, because it is so difficult to do so with the current market size. Thus, we advocate public investment to boost the market size so that local business owners can run their operations to generate profits and to create other local employment opportunities, while still providing a service that locals can utilize as well. To go further, we believe that nurturing this local entrepreneurial spirit is one of the conditions necessary to sustain rural tourism, and in turn, to sustain rural communities and to justify the investment of public funds that we advocate (see also McElwee and Whittam, 2012)

The Role of Government: To Be a Catalyst

At a time where traditional small-scale fishing and farming employment has been wounded by technological change and global competition, rural communities need to find a way to develop economic activities that are compatible with the skills, interests, preferences, and needs of its citizens. Based on a review of available literature and our own field research, we believe that investing in tourism, culturally-based or otherwise, is a practical option. To be blunt, it cannot realistically happen without the injection of public funds to lead the charge. Policy makers are integral to the workability of a viable tourism industry in rural communities because it is policy makers who can develop and maintain the infrastructure that drives tourist volume in a community. For example, our Fogo Island and Trinity Bight research appears to indicate that some tourists reacted negatively to the current level of infrastructure like roads, signage or activities. Yet, it is infeasible to expect an individual business owner, or even one local community, to bear the financial burden of trying to grow an industry for the benefit of all.

The stark choice is either to let rural communities slowly dwindle or to intercede and sustain those communities by boosting incomes directly or indirectly. With that in mind, it would seem that the choices are between handouts in the form of social assistance, or a path to sustainability. We, of course, argue for the latter, because it avoids a reliance on income support measures for community sustainability. Investment in tourism is not an option that we expect to provide a rash of good quality jobs in rural communities. Instead, seasonal employment is the first goal, to be followed later by opportunities for small businesses to enter, as customer counts grow. On Fogo Island in Newfoundland, the Shorefast Foundation and its founding benefactor acted as the catalyst. They are well-funded, passionate, highly focused and capable, well connected politically, and intent on using a social entrepreneurial approach to expand tourism and related industries in the area via a close connection to the historical and cultural traditions. Yet, even with that strategic intent, there is some opposition as people worry about a potential change to the local way of life. Of course, when a long distance from larger urban centers, too many communities are facing dangerously low population levels. On Fogo Island, something bold needed to be done, and there needed to be an injection of funds. Tourism simply could not reach sustainable levels without a long-term financial commitment, and a vision of how to attract visitors to this beautiful, yet remote, area. In our other example, Trinity Bight, locals made the decision to retain and celebrate their architecture and business traditions by communally owning important buildings in the community center. Yet, they still require annual funding from multiple levels of government to operate their museums and theater, which, in turn, fills their B&Bs and shops.

We view both of these communities as being on the road to tourist success, because public investments have been made. In our recent technical report (i.e. Cooke, Burns, and McManamon, 2013), we summarized the empirical evidence indicating that investing in rural tourism – if done correctly – can stimulate regional economic development as well as enriching the social and cultural lives of local citizens. The 'catch' is that effectiveness of public investments cannot be measured merely in financial terms. Other factors are needed to provide a fuller picture. These include an expanded economic base, repopulation, social improvement, and revitalization of local crafts. Additionally, the cash flows created by rural tourism can assist in job retention in services such as retailing, transport, hospitality and medical care (Irshad, 2010). Rural tourism can also assist in diversifying income sources in climatically marginal regions, and aid in environmental improvements and landscape conservation that can provide jobs in maintaining and repairing traditional landscapes and areas worn by recreational activities (Irshad, 2010). Policy makers should consider these less measurable benefits when assessing the viability of investment in tourism in rural communities. Nonetheless, the investments need to be large enough to generate a critical mass of available tourist attractions and activities, so that potential visitors make the decision to venture to a more remote location for a vacation (Constantin and Mitrut, 2009; Cooke, Burns, and McManamon, 2013). Ironically, then, to improve the chances of generating a return, the investment of public funds must be large and sustained enough to attract tangibly more visitors.

Canadian governments and affiliates who are seeking ways to implement sustainable forms of development at the local level, especially in rural areas, should focus on the creation and maintenance of festivals and other cultural events that can extend the typical tourist season. These initiatives not only generate revenue for governments, they also have positive economic impacts on the local economy by generating income, supporting existing businesses, and encouraging new start-ups. The creation of entry-level tourism industry positions makes it easier for discouraged or unemployed workers to enter this field with only moderate levels of training, potentially of the on-the-job variety (Cooke, Burns, and McManamon, 2013; Elkin and Roberts, 1994). Rural regions located close to urban centers may provide an opportunity to take advantage of these nearby markets to generate an increase in rural tourism employment.

In order for rural tourism initiatives to be successful, proper infrastructure needs to be in place to support these initiatives (e.g. Constantin and Mitrut, 2009). Government investments would need to include improving roads and transportation systems, improving signage, parks and recreation, preservation of heritage buildings, supporting existing community events, expanding the availability, access and quality of existing attractions, developing new attractions and events, and stretching the tourist season into shoulder months (see Cooke, Burns, and McManamon, 2013; Irshad, 2010). If undertaken strategically, there is also the opportunity of improving the quality of life of locals not involved in tourism - if the types of visitor segments and visitor activities that are developed mesh with the interests and lifestyles of the local citizens. We again return to an earlier theme. There is a need for public funding to be used to improve the infrastructure to get to rural communities (via road improvements or public transportation), to enhance the physical infrastructure to make a visit to rural communities more enjoyable (via signage, parking, visitors centers, etc), to create and operate events (like festivals or theatres or parks) and to allow existing attractions (like museums and tourist offices) to remain open during off-peak parts of the year. Governments need to be the catalyst to stretch and deepen tourist seasons. In Fogo Island, if the ferry service is the bottleneck preventing more tourists traffic in peak season, only governments are in a position to make improvements. If, in places like Trinity Bight, B&Bs and museums and boat operators shut down for the season because nothing else is open and the tourists have stopped coming, then governments must act by keeping museums and tourist centers open, so that tourists still enjoy coming, which, in turn, will provide incentives for B&Bs and cafes to stay open as well. Not surprisingly, many governments and observers have been focused on ways to attract those incremental customers to stretch the tourist season, and boost revenues and rural employment (e.g. Government of NL, 2009; Government of PEI, 2010; Cooke, Burns, and McManamon, 2013; Irshad, 2010), although we believe that bolder action is required.

CONCLUSION

Given the economic restructuring that has occurred due to globalization, demographic trends, and economic policy shifts, the reality in the indus-trialized world is that jobs are less stable and secure as employers react to the new conditions and look for operational efficiencies. Moreover, the situation is potentially more acute in remote, rural areas which have to adapt to these supra-national pressures while also coping with declining and aging populations, and struggles in the traditional pastimes of small-scale fishing and farming. For better or worse, the tourism industry is frequently where community officials, bureaucrats, and citizens are pinning their hopes for the future vitality of rural areas. On the one hand, a rural tourism industry requires substantial capital investment and a long-term commitment of public funds, and likely to yield mainly low-paying, seasonal jobs. Nonetheless, these jobs - if appearing with enough certainty and for enough months a year on an annual basis- can potentially meet the needs of some segments of the rural labour force.

The purpose of this chapter was to present the role that tourism could and should play within rural communities as a means of economic diversification and stimulation. Two examples from the Canadian province of Newfoundland and Labrador were used in our analysis. The more one studies 'rural' people, the more one grasps the diversity – in terms of economic circumstances, politics and social views, attitudes, family situations, lifestyles, and history, to name a few – within rural communities. On the other hand, when comparing to the circumstances facing urban citizens, it is necessary to utilize some broad generalizations. The labour markets of near-urban and suburban communities essentially operate as urban ones. Conversely, small communities that are remote are the ones that truly have 'rural' labour markets.

In generations past, individual workers were subject to economic cycles. In good times, jobs were easy to find and retain, and money was more plentiful. In down times, employment opportunities decreased in number, and individuals and families would feel the financial pinch. In the past couple decades, however, it would seem that a change has occurred. While there are intermittently strong and weak periods within economic cycles, the notion of 'jobless recoveries' has entered the public discussion. Also, one must now consider the level of casual, on-call, temporary, fixed-term, and part-time jobs in Canada, the United States, and elsewhere in the industrialized world.

Rural economies, when remotely located from urban centers, tend to contain weaker and fewer employment options. On the whole, though, older people tend to be quite content with their lives even if employment prospects are limited, but those people still need at least a minimum level of employment income to be able to remain in their hometowns. This implies that, for older rural individuals, the public policy goal should be to spread available public funds thinly. That is, the objective should be to maximize the coverage of public funds to as many individuals within as many needy communities as possible. The result would be to provide a basic level of income support (via seasonal, and/or part-time), but in a manner that is dignified, practical, and efficient, to sustain individual households within rural communities. The reality of the tourism industry in rural areas is that it is much more likely to feature seasonal employment. Thus, we would argue that employment in this industry is primarily suited to older rural individuals looking for any annual opportunities for paid work, or for the young adults who want any available local employment, rather than for young rural adults who are seeking skills/acquisition first, and then upward mobility second.

We recognize that critics will argue that spending public funds to develop tourist in rural areas will only waste taxpayers' money. We counter that tourism is one of the few options where employment can be sustainable, and where the investment of public funds can help to entice visitors while also improving the quality of life for local citizens. It is true that not every rural community is going to be a draw for tourists. However, many places with natural beauty, and social and cultural significance, and a communal willingness to embrace visitors can have enough tourism to spawn opportunities ranging from seasonal employment to opportunities to run a business; an oft overlooked point. Once one separates rural labour forces into young workers and older workers, and looks at the different motivations and career stages of these two groups (on average) tourism begins to look like a good fit. That said, it is not an easy or quick solution. There are also no guarantees for success. In fact, without a community champion, or if lacking a critical mass of activities, or if too small, too remote, or if simply lacking in appeal to visitors, a rural community is unlikely to be able to generate a sustainable tourism industry.

Tourism, while requiring an ongoing and significant level of investment in infrastructure, marketing, and human resources, can lead to self-employment and paid employment possibilities for a range of different types of workers. It is important to differentiate between urban, near urban (or suburban), and truly rural (i.e. small and with at least some degree of remoteness from the nearest urban center). In truly rural settings, it is a necessity that governments lead the charge by investing public funds into tourism to spur on community efforts to develop this industry, and to set the stage for private sector operators to then take opportunities to get involved as well. On Fogo Island in Newfoundland, the Shorefast Foundation acted as the catalyst, but they also have access to public funds to implement their vision. In Trinity Bight, a grass-roots community initiative protected the architecture and business traditions of their communities, and then leveraged public sector funds to attract visitors to a range of local arts options. In both (sets of) communities, tourism is not yet self-sustaining, yet both offer a path towards future economic sustainability, as long as governments are willing to commit to long-term funding to support tourism. In both communities, there is some nervousness and skepticism among locals about the likelihood of being able to rely on employment in tourism, and how tourism might impact local lifestyles and traditions. On the other hand, there was almost universal agreement that if governments 'do nothing, then the result will be declining and slowly dying communities. Given this reality, readers of this chapter should consider: if the tourism industry is not developed, then what will be the savior of these rural communities, given today's labour markets and global competition? Tourism requires ongoing investments and a developed infrastructure, but for communities without natural resources to develop, or without enough profitable manufacturing or primary industries, tourism at least offers reasonable prospects for the future.

In this era of austerity budgets, governments can be tempted to cut services to, and programs for, rural areas, much less make long-term funding commitments to grow tourism. Moreover, investing in rural tourism infrastructure can be especially daunting to governments because economic rates of return only document part of the possible benefits. It is also necessary to look at social elements like well-being, community vibrancy, and feelings of accomplishment. If one looks critically at the public policy alternatives, we believe that investing in tourism offers reasonable prospects for diversifying and sustaining rural economies. We think that governments must face a two-pronged decision. The first is whether or not to utilize public funds to sustain rural communities. If not, many of those communities will reach an economic and demographic point of no return in which decline is inevitable. On the other hand, if utilizing public funds is the choice, then the second decision is whether to give handouts (i.e. direct income supports) or to invest in the communities (i.e. tourism) to develop sustainable economies. Based on those options, we see substantial merit with investing in tourism for the economic and social benefits that can accrue. To make our case, we have intentionally relied on two somewhat obscure community examples in Canada's most easterly province of Newfoundland, both of which illustrate the benefits, challenges, and public investments required to develop rural tourism. While the road ahead is unclear, we believe that the prospects for sustainability are good, and the decision to rely on tourism warranted.

REFERENCES

Alasia, A. (2010). Population Change Across Canadian Communities, 1981 to 2006, The Role of Sector Restructuring, Agglomeration, Diversification and Human Capital. Rural and Small Town Canada Analysis Bulletin 8(4):1-25. Statistics Canada Catalogue number 21-006-X.

Bernard, A., Finnie, R. and St.-Jean, B. (2008). "Interprovincial Mobility and Earnings," *Perspectives on Labour and Income* 9, No. 10: 15-25, Statistics Canada Catalogue No. 75-001-X.

Betcherman, G, and Lowe, G.S. . (1997). *The Future of Work in Canada: A Synthesis Report.* Canadian Policy Research Networks. 57 p. http://www.cprn.org/documents/24985_en.pdf (accessed June 8, 2009).

Burns, J. K. (2012). Employment preferences of millennial nursing graduates in Newfoundland & Labrador. MER Project, Memorial University of Newfoundland.

Canadian Council on Learning [CCL]. (2006). The rural-urban gap in education.

Accessed January 1, 2012. www.ccl-cca.ca/pdfs/LessonsInLearning/10-03_01_06E.pdf.

Chaykowski, R.P. and Gunderson, M. (2001). The implications of globalization for labour and labour markets. In R.P. Chaykowski (Ed.), *Globalization and the Canadian Economy: The Implications for Labour Markets, Society and the State* (pp. 27-60). Kingston, CAN: School of Policy Studies, Queen's University.

Constantin, D.L. and Mitrut, C. 2009. Cultural tourism, sustainability and regional development: experiences from Romania. In Cultural Tourism and Sustainable Local development (Girard, L.F. and Nijkamp, P, eds). Ashgate: UK; 149-166.

Cooke, G.B. (2007). Alternative work schedules and related issues among Atlantic Canadians. *The Workplace Review*, 4(2), 8-15. Sobey School of Business at Saint Mary's University.

Cooke, G.B. (2012). High Fliers versus Upstream Swimmers: Young rural workers in Canada and Ireland. In *Youth Unemployment and Joblessness: Causes, Consequences, Responses*: 151-168. Association for International and Comparative Studies in the field of Labour law and Industrial Relations (ADAPT). Cambridge Scholars Publishing. ISBN (10): 1-4438-4056-4 & ISBN (13): 978-1-4438-4056-4

Cooke, G.B., Burns, J.K., and McManamon, D. K. (2013). The Case for Public Investment in Cultural Tourism in Gros Morne National Park (GMNP). Prepared for Atlantic Canada Opportunities Agency, Newfoundland and Labrador.

Cooke, G.B., Donaghey, J., and Zeytinoglu, I.U. (2013). The nuanced nature of work quality: evidence from rural Newfoundland and Ireland. *Human Relations,* 66(4), 503-527.

Cooke, G.B., Zeytinoglu, I.U., Mann, S.L., and Chowhan, J. (2012). Trends in Work Schedules among Key Worker Sub-groups in Canada. Statistics Canada RDC Working Paper Series, No. 42. This report is available at http://socserv.mcmaster.ca/rdc/RDCwp42.pdf.

Cooke, G.B., Zeytinoglu, I.U., Agarwal, N., and Rose, J.B. (2008). Employee-friendly and employer-friendly non-standard work schedules and locations. *International Journal of Employment Studies, 16(2),* 31-66.

Cooke, G.B. and Mann, S.L. (2011). Young rural workers, the pursuit of education, and employment opportunities: Canadian and Irish perspectives - A tale of two studies. Presented at the North Atlantic Forum, St. John's, Newfoundland and Labrador.

Elkin, R.D., and Roberts, R.S. 1994. Crafting a destination vision. In Travel, Tourism, and Hospitality Research: A handbook for managers and Researchers (Ritchie, J.R.B., and Goeldner, C.R., eds.). Wiley and Sons: US; 403-412.

Freshwater, D. (2008). Rural Urban Interaction NL: Understanding and managing Regions. Municipalities Newfoundland and Labrador. Retrieved from: http://www.municipalitiesNLcom/userfiles/files/ALMP%20low%20 res.pdf on 21 August 2013.

Government of Canada [Government of Canada]. 2013. Labour Market Bulletin - Newfoundland and Labrador: 2012 (Annual Edition). Prepared by the Labour market information (LMI) Division of the *Human Resources and Skills Development Canada (HRSDC).* Downloaded from http://www.hrsdc.gc.ca/eng/jobs/lmi/publications/bulletins/nfld/annual201 2.shtml on August 31, 2013.

Government of Newfoundland and Labrador [Government of NL]. N.d. Tourism research Frequently Asked Questions. Downloaded from website of the Department of Tourism, Culture, and Recreation. http://www. tcr.gov.nl.ca/tcr/faq/tourism_statistics.html on 21 August 2013.

Government of Newfoundland and Labrador [Government of NL]. 2009. *Uncommon Potential: A Vision for Newfoundland and Labrador Tourism.* Retrieved from http://www.tcr.gov.nl.ca/tcr/publications/2009/Vision_2020_Print_Text.pdf

Government of Prince Edward Island [Government of PEI]. 2010. *Rural Action Plan: A Rural Economic Development Strategy for Prince Edward Island: One Island Community.* Rural Development PEI, Department of Fisheries, Aquaculture and Rural Development.

Irshad, H. (2010). Rural Tourism- An Overview. Government of Alberta Agriculture and Rural Development report. Downloaded from http://www1.agric.gov.ab.ca/$department/deptdocs.nsf/all/csi13476 on August 19, 2013.

Kochan, T.A., Katz, H.C. and McKersie, R.B. (1986) *The Transformation of American Industrial Relations.* NY, US: Basic Books.

Lagravinese, R. 2012. Rural tourism and ancient traditions: Evidence from Italian regions. *Local Economy*, 27(2), 614-626.

McElwee, G. and Whittam, G. 2012. A sustainable rural? *Local Economy*, 27(2), 91-94.

Organisation for Economic Co-operation and Development [OECD]. (2006). Reinventing rural policy. Policy brief.

Saunders, R. (2003). *Defining Vulnerability in the Labour Market.* Vulnerable Workers Series. No. 1. November. Canadian Policy Research Networks. 24 p.http://www.cprn.org/documents/25148_en.pdf (accessed July 10, 2009).

Shorefast Foundation. (2013). Miscellaneous website information down loaded, on Aug 1 2013, from http://www.shorefast.org/ .

Timothy, D.J. (2011). Cultural heritage and tourism: An introduction. Channel View Publications: UK. Chapter 1: Cultural heritage and tourism: 1-11.

Raj, R. (2003). The impact of festivals on cultural tourism. *The 2nd DeHaan Tourism Management Conference "Developing Cultural Tourism"*, December 16, 2003.

Trinity Historical Society. (2013). Miscellaneous website information downloaded, on Aug 1 2013, from http://www. Trinityhistoricalsociety.com/ .

Vallée, G. (2005). *Towards Enhancing the Employment Conditions of Vulnerable Workers: A Public Policy Perspective.* Vulnerable Workers Series. No. 2. March. Canadian Policy Research Networks. 57 p. http://www.cprn.ca/documents/35588_en.pdf (accessed July 10, 2009).

Verma, A., and Chaykowski, R.P. (1999). Employment and employment relations at the crossroads. In Contract and Commitment: Employment Relations in the New Economy, edited by Anil Verma, and Richard P. Chaykowski, 1-20. Kingston, ON: IRC Press, Queen's University.

Zeytinoglu, I.U., Cooke, G.B., and Mann, S.L. (2009). Flexibility: whose choice is it anyway? *Relations Industrielles/Industrial Relations,* 64(4), 555-574.

In: Labor Markets
Editor: William E. Grossman

ISBN: 978-1-62948-662-8
© 2014 Nova Science Publishers, Inc.

Chapter 3

CHALLENGING GLOBALIZATION: AN EXTENSION OF A THEORY OF MARGINALITY UTILIZING THE CASE OF PUBLIC SCHOOL TEACHERS IN THE DOMINICAN REPUBLIC

Karie Jo Peralta and George Wilson*
University of Miami, Miami, Florida, US

ABSTRACT

This chapter builds on Torres's (2009) theory of "marginality" in understanding how socioeconomic inequality generated by a neoliberal form of globalization can be challenged and ultimately, more equitable outcomes can ensue. Specifically, based on extensive field work in which we utilize teachers' struggle in the Dominican Republic for better livelihoods, we add three tenets to Torres' theory: (1) Pursuing social transformation requires the incorporation of the poor; (2) The marginalized are responsible for integrating others who are socially excluded in transformative social justice learning practices; and, (3) The marginalized have the ability to initiate the creation of a world free of social inequalities, that, when viewed through the lens of a "trans-

---

* Corresponding author: Karie Jo Peralta, PhD Student, Department of Sociology, University of Miami. Merrick Building, Coral Gables, Florida 33146. E-mail: k.peralta@miami.edu.

formative social justice learning" rationale moves forward an agenda that provides a more equitable outcome from globalization processes. We conclude by discussing how this critical agenda can be further developed in subsequent research.

INTRODUCTION

Scholars in the area of international development (e.g. Kapoor, 2011; Ruccio, 2011; Veltmeyer, 2014) have now critiqued the current form of neoliberal globalization for over 20 years (for a review, see Applebaum and Robinson, 2005). In this regard, critics have been especially critical of the consequences of globalization in the spheres of work and education, specifically citing the progressively widening gap between the rich and poor and fundamental lack of status and dignity of workers. These outcomes, in fact, are viewed as a result of a form of globalization predicated on well-documented tenets of 21st century neoliberalism that prioritizes laissez-faire principles, such as unfettered markets, open and free competition, and minimal state intervention. Overall, globalization processes in their neoliberal incarnation are viewed by critics as justifying a form of exploitive capitalism, which, ultimately, disproportionately advantages those in power at the expense of the rest of society.

Significantly, in contrast to the rhetoric of advocates of a contemporary neoliberal form of globalization (Bhagwati, 2004), critics maintain these forms of inequality that result in high rates of impoverishment and alienation is not the result of natural processes nor is it an inevitable by-product of economic relations; they can, in fact, be altered, thereby enhancing the life-chance opportunity status and dignity of the disenfranchised (Atasoy and Carroll, 2003; Esposito, 2009; Torres, 2009). Along these lines, recognizing that globalization can take multiple forms, these critics --whose perspective is grounded in Critical Social Theory (Adorno, Frankel-Brunswick, Levinson, and Nevitt Sanford, 1950; Habermas, 1984; Horkheimer and Adorno, 1972; Marcuse, 1964), --challenge "top-down" globalization, that is globalization that privileges multinational corporations and global leaders in world markets and elevates the status of the market with the claim that free, open, and unfettered competition is in the best interests of and benefits everyone. Overall, the project for those critical of neoliberal globalization is to illuminate, based on sound theory, visions and practices that contribute to the development of humanizing forms of globalization "from below," (Murphy,

2004; Torres, 2009) that is globalization that develops from local level concerns (Brecher, Costello, and Smith, 2000).

Carlos Alberto Torres (2009), a political sociologist, recently proposed a theory of "marginality" applicable to Paulo Freire's (1970) practice of "transformative social justice learning" as a strategy that can be used to construct an alternative to a neoliberal form of globalization. Torres (2009) delineates a number of tenets that constitute a way to develop an alternative logic of globalization. He maintains that power relationships in educational institutions shape forms of cultural reproduction and economic relationships that, in turn, structure life-chance opportunities (Bernstein, 1977; Bourdieu and Passeron, 1977; Bowles and Gintis, 1976). This chapter attempts to further develop this critical agenda. It builds on Torres's (2009) theory of marginality, specifically, by adding three tenets to a "transformative social justice learning" agenda as a way of moving toward an approach that provides more equitable outcomes of globalization. Based on four years of extensive field work, service-learning, and volunteer experience collaborating with public school teachers and students pursuing teaching careers in poor, rural communities in the Dominican Republic, we present the case of public school teachers in the Dominican Republic as a case study, analyzing their demands for increased salaries and benefits via the campaign, "Dignifying the Teaching Profession." In doing so, we identify globalization generated barriers that preclude fuller participation in the development of policy related to their profession. In particular, we identify their marginalized status, which leaves them out of discourse on issues related to their professional lives.

The chapter unfolds as follows: The first section, "A Developing Theory of Marginality," provides an overview of Torres' (2009) theory of marginality. The second section, "Historical and Contemporary Context of the Dominican Republic," describes the historical development of the Dominican Republic and focuses on the teaching profession and teachers' struggles. The third section, "An Extension of a Theory of Marginality," delineates an extended version of a theory of marginality utilizing the teachers' movement in the Dominican Republic. The final section, "Directions for Future Research," identifies areas in need of further inquiry that will advance an agenda that is critical of neoliberal globalization and necessary for the empowerment of teachers in the Dominican Republic. Our elaboration incorporates poverty, the socially excluded, and the ability the marginalized have to initiate change. We hope this intellectual excursion will demonstrate that theoretical insights generated from multiple disciplines can be utilized to gain critical insight into possibilities for action against a neoliberal form of globalization.

A DEVELOPING THEORY OF MARGINALITY

Torres' (2009) theory of marginality represents the foremost critique of the consequences of neoliberal globalization. In fact, the contribution of Torres' work, firmly entrenched in the Marxist-inspired tradition of Critical Social Theory (Adorno et al., 1950, Habermas, 1984; Horkheimer and Adorno, 1972; Marcuse, 1964), constitutes an analytic framework or guide for action thus constituting "praxis" in the Marxist sense.

In particular, it adopts Freire's (1970) notion of "transformative social justice learning," which involves individuals in an action-oriented, reflective process that calls for "crossing borders," that is developing the capacity to analyze and understand own and other's socially, culturally, and politically formed modes of thought through dialogue as a way of addressing issues relating to democratic participation and diversity.

The tenets of Torres' (2009) theory of marginality are as follows:

(1) Pursuing social change requires utilizing theory that differs from the dominant Western tradition of logical positivism.

(2) Promoting social justice from a marginalized position includes recognizing achievements of overcoming obstacles in the struggle against oppression and exploitation, as well as, the challenges that persist in creating equality.

(3) Marginality constitutes a theory of knowledge that is a basis for political consciousness.

(4) The marginalized are responsible for engaging in social movements and establishing a position to participate in public debates.

(5) Employing transformative social justice learning practices involves searching for alternative versions of a world characterized by equality and solidarity.

The first tenet addresses the relegation of transformative social justice learning to a role of non-significance in dialogue on social change, which ultimately, marginalizes those who employ it within academic and non-academic settings. Along these lines, Torres (2009) emphasizes that scholars engaged in transformative social justice learning are marginalized because they reject the tenets of logical positivism (see Guba and Lincoln, 1994; Torres, 2009), the dominant paradigm in social scientific and education research. Specifically, they reject "objective reality," the discovery of value-free facts, and the belief that the human condition must be overcome in knowledge production. Instead, these scholars employ Critical Social Theory, which grounds knowledge of the social order in historical, social processes and contemporary contexts influenced by the historically contingent nature of capitalism (Horkheimer, 1972).

The second tenet of a theory of marginality offers critical possibilities for a more humane society, though it is recognized that achieving a better world will not be easy. In particular, it views the active engaging in discourse as a celebrated achievement in social transformation and results in a form of empowerment, in which the status of being marginal is transformed into a dignified and honorable status. The third tenet in the theory of marginality entails awareness of how marginality constitutes a theory of knowledge. The knowledge base, in fact, is not abhorrent or extreme in terms of its being removed from "mainstream values and orientations," but a basis for a specific form of political consciousness. This consciousness yields an advantage in ascertaining how education or educational philosophy, as promoted by Freire (1970), is fundamentally political and can be shaped accordingly.

The fourth tenet calls for individuals to be active in social movements and engage in public debates. In this regard, Torres (2009) views as particularly crucial, "reclaiming the transformative role of teachers as public intellectuals, and of teachers' unions and social movements in the context of defending public education as a foundation of the social democratic pact" (p. 94). Applied to this study, this belief translates into regaining the position of teachers and supporters of public education in debates, ultimately, bringing them into view as a force in educational politics. Finally, the fifth tenet of the marginality theory entails the search for alternative versions of a world free of inequalities and oppression, which involves envisioning and striving for an ideal model of society from a perspective of the marginalized. Importantly, the search for other modes of existence requires intentional thought processes followed by action. The strategy to realize a particular utopian model is employing a theory of marginality with the practice of transformative social justice learning (Torres, 2009). Overall, the theory of marginality must be viewed as operating within a historically contingent global setting.

All together, these tenets guide the search for alternatives to neoliberal globalization and pushes forward the transformative social justice learning agenda, but do not provide a basis for exploring and integrating into the discourse the concerns of the poor and socially isolated who are populations that could benefit most from a just society. Additionally, Torres' (2009) theory is limited by not conveying a central notion of the marginalized as capable of initiating social change. We recognize that the theory is helpful in framing the experiences of teachers in the Dominican Republic, but our additional tenets allow for a deeper understanding of their struggle for empowerment and illuminate a path towards new possibilities to mobilize and improve their livelihoods. We now describe the Dominican Republic case with an emphasis on elaborating the current context of school teachers as marginalized subjects.

HISTORICAL AND CONTEMPORARY CONTEXT OF THE DOMINICAN REPUBLIC

Dominican Republic in the Global System

The transition to world capitalism has transformed virtually every country in the globe. Of course, the Dominican case is no exception. The Dominican Republic's economy was based on cattle-ranching and tobacco, sugar, and wood-cutting industries after gaining independence from Haiti in 1844 and as a Spanish colony throughout the years 1861-1865. Once independence was restored, different authoritarian regimes gained power in distinct regions of the country and took advantage of liberties to obtain foreign loans. High debts ensued and financial and political instability eventually led to foreign intervention (Martínez Vergne, 2005; Moya Pons, 1998).

The United States intervened to bring political and financial stability to the Dominican Republic on two occasions from the years 1916-1924 and 1964-1965 (Moya Pons, 1998). Between the two US occupations, Rafael Leónidas Trujillo promoted modernization in agriculture and manufacturing during his thirty-one year dictatorship. After the 1970s, the economy shifted from being based on sugar production to manufacturing and tourism, but jobs vanished due to the increase in technology. The government encouraged migration to the United States as a result of high unemployment (Torres-Saillant and Hernández, 1998). Immigrant remittances supplemented family incomes as unemployment rates continued to increase (Organisation for Economic Co-operation and Development, 2008).

The Dominican Republic officially entered the global arena via the World Trade Organization in the year 1995, which later resulted in the 2004 Dominican Republic-Central America-United States Free Trade Agreement. Although many international companies opened factories in the free zones, jobs were short-lived due to increasing competition from Asian countries in the early 2000s (The Stop CAFTA Coalition, 2007). Today, the economy is based on the service industry, specifically tourism, but also continues to be largely supported by remittances (Central Intelligence Agency, 2013).

The historical instability of the country's politics and economy underpins the current conditions of Dominican society. Recent reports identify various social problems: high level of poverty (World Bank, 2013b); high rate of unemployment; low wages; low labor force participation (International Labor Organization, 2011); poor quality of education; high illiteracy rate (Gajardo, 2007); high rate of teenage pregnancy (Center of Social and Demographic Studies, 2007); high level of public perceptions of government corruption (Transparency International, 2012); high rate of domestic violence (Center of Social and Demographic Studies, 2007); poor quality of public healthcare services (Pan American Health Organization, 2007); racial discrimination (United Nations Human Rights Council, 2008); and a high rate of child labor (Office of National Statistics of the Dominican Republic, 2011). These contemporary issues characterize a social context of inequality, exploitation, and oppression.

The Sphere of Education in the Dominican Republic

In 1845, after one year of independence, lawmakers established the foundation of the Dominican public education system. One of the most significant figures in the development of the education system, particularly in the training of teachers, is Eugenio María de Hostos who was born in Puerto Rico, studied in Spain, and advocated for social justice issues and education throughout Latin America. In 1880, María de Hostos opened the first Normal School in the Dominican Republic, more commonly known as a teachers college. More than a century later, the Normal School continues to function in the country as an institution where high school graduates can earn a teaching certificate (Organisation for Economic Co-operation and Development, 2008).

The education system was further developed during the first US occupation and was established similar to the American education system, which endured with minimal adjustments until the 1990s. In order to respond to severe disparities in education, the Ministry of Education created the Ten-Year Educational Plan from 1992-2002. This plan intended to guide the improvement of teacher training, curriculum, resources, and vocational education. However, many of the reforms were not fully implemented and objectives were not completely met (Organisation for Economic Co-operation and Development, 2008). Other ten-year educational plans for the years 2003-

2012 and 2008-2018 have been produced with continued goals of increasing quality and access (State Secretary of Education of the Dominican Republic, 2008).

One of the major public arguments for why the quality of education in the Dominican Republic is poor has been that the government has not upheld the General Law of Education (66-97) established in 1997. This law requires that the government invest 4% of the country's Gross Domestic Product (GDP) or 16% of the national budget in education (State Secretary of Education of the Dominican Republic, 1997). However, the government has never complied with this law, and instead has invested in projects intended to increase the country's competitiveness in the world market, thereby making neoliberal globalization a significant influence on the country's development. In 2007, the public expenditure on education reached just 2.2% of the GDP (World Bank, 2013a). Mobilization began in the year 2010 to raise public awareness of this issue through the "4% for Education" movement. After many national marches, protests, and campaign events, the newly elected president in 2012, Danilo Medina Sánchez, announced that he would fulfill his campaign promise by investing 4% of the GDP beginning in 2013 (Listin Diario, 2012).

The Struggle to Dignify the Teaching Profession

The success of the "4% for Education" movement has fueled the teachers' union, the Dominican Association of Teachers, to fight for a 100% salary increase for public school teachers, better benefits for retired and pensioned educators, and more complete health coverage for teachers and their families. In a country where more than 40% of the population is living in poverty (World Bank, 2013b), teachers in the Dominican Republic have consistently voiced that a dignified salary will help to lift them out of impoverishment. The dignity that they are reclaiming relates to teachers being able to afford basic living needs, such as providing food for their family, covering their children's medical expenses, and purchasing decent attire to wear to work.

To shed light on the economic situation of teachers, the average teacher's salary is approximately $219 per month. However, the living wage for a worker of a family of four who has a second wage earner is nearly $498 per month (Worker Rights Consortium, 2008). Thus, the average teachers' salary does not meet half the living wage for a "typical" family.

Based on those dynamics, the Dominican Association of Teachers is currently leading the nation's teachers in the campaign, "Dignifying the

Teaching Profession." For months teachers have demonstrated in support of the campaign (Acevedo, 2013; Despertar Dominicano, 2013). In fact, their conviction is manifest as recently as five months ago after rejecting the government's announcement of providing a 20% increase in salaries (Jorge, 2013). They have since organized a march to the State Secretary of Education to demand that the government uphold the laws of the Dominican education system (Ciudadoriental.org, 2013) and continue to make their claims known in the media (Dominican Today, 2013). Although teachers have utilized peaceful methods of mobilization, the government criticized them for holding a 48-hour strike, which affected students because classes were not held (Diario Libre, 2013). To this date, teachers persist in the struggle for their dignity and are receiving increasing support from educational organizations around the world (Assunção, 2011).

AN EXTENSION OF THE THEORY OF MARGINALITY

The three additional tenets that we delineate take into account the struggles of public school teachers in the Dominican Republic as they continue to live in conditions of poverty while they at the same time experience a lack of recognition for their work in educating the country's youth. These tenets underscore the importance of solidarity among teachers across the nation if they are to be successful in developing alternatives to the neoliberal globalization processes that impact their livelihoods. Each tenet is important for the empowerment of teachers as integral members of society and for claiming their dignity as professional leaders of the Dominican Republic.

Incorporating the Position of the Poor

The first additional tenet we offer in the theory of marginality is that pursuing social transformation requires the incorporation of the poor.

Including the poor would provide a perspective of the barriers that prevent the poor from using their agency to counter globalization. Keeping with the Freirian tradition of viewing the world from the position of the marginalized, we apply our tenet of the theory of marginality to examine the need for public school teachers in the Dominican Republic to gain additional training as a result of the Dominican government calling for teachers to better prepare students to enter the labor force and increase the country's competitiveness in the global market. The government provides an option for teachers to increase their salary by completing advanced training. Unlike many school districts in the United States that offer to pay for teachers to return to school to earn specialized certificates and degrees, teachers in the Dominican Republic have to pay for additional schooling out of their own salaries. Because universities are located only in major towns, teachers from rural communities have to plan for long, costly commutes. For some teachers, the time and costs involved with pursuing additional education could outweigh the incentives. For those living in severe conditions of poverty and with significant family commitments, the possibility to further their education is bleak. Consequently, teachers can argue that the government's call for teachers to obtain advanced degrees must be supported first by a general increase in salaries.

By addressing poverty-related barriers that impede teachers from gaining upward mobility, the theory contributes to an explanation of why achieving justice requires a determined effort. Furthermore, this additional tenet helps to recognize the lack of power of those living in conditions of poverty. Thus, if marginality involves a political struggle, as Torres (2009) makes clear, utilizing the perspective of the poor in transformative social justice learning would allow teachers to identify how they could be empowered by connecting with thousands of Dominicans who live in poverty to increase their support and, in turn, pressure government officials to acknowledge that they are worthy of receiving salary increases.

Reaching the Socially Isolated

The second tenet we contribute to the theory of marginality is the marginalized are responsible for integrating others who are socially excluded in transformative social justice learning practices. In the spirit of Freire's work with Brazilian peasants, we examine how teachers living in rural regions are at a disadvantage in participating in the "Dignifying the Teaching Profession" campaign.

Because the Dominican government often overlooks rural community issues to invest in projects that will develop the country's economy, the teachers' union should make involving rural teachers in the campaign a priority so that they can contribute their voices to the debate. We maintain that this tenet is important specifically to increase support and unify teachers across the country in promoting the campaign. Rural teachers experience significant isolation from their peers making it difficult for them to access information regarding the campaign and integrate into the movement.

In fact, the Dominican Association of Teachers is based in Santo Domingo, the capital city located on the south coast, and most campaign activities occur there. Demonstrations have typically taken place outside the State Secretary of Education building, also located in Santo Domingo. Therefore, teachers living in or near the capital city are more likely than teachers living in rural regions to be informed about and participate in the campaign. Nevertheless, rural teachers are important stakeholders in the movement and should have the opportunity to be involved in the campaign.

The Dominican Association of Teachers is one of 199 organizations, agencies, and institutions that comprise the Dignified Education Coalition, which is the flagship entity of the "4% for Education" movement that peacefully demands that the government invest 4% of the country's GDP in education as stated by the General Law of Education (66-97) (State Secretary of Education of the Dominican Republic 1997). The Coalition has garnered the support of the Dominican population, as well as, of organizations across Latin America. In fact, on March 4, 2011, more than 200 organizations from 20 different countries demonstrated their solidarity by presenting a petition backing the movement to the Dominican Republic's embassy in each respective country (Assunção, 2011). As a nation-wide Coalition, its network is important for transmitting the demands of the teachers across the Dominican Republic. Recently, the Coalition has not only created awareness of the government's commitment to investing in education and whether 4% of the GDP will be spent by the year 2014, but has also alerted the public that the government must involve all sectors of society in education planning.

In fact, it was reported on August 22, 2013 that the Coalition announced that by President Medina not inviting the Coalition to a meeting on reforms, the government had excluded citizens and organizations in the interior of the Dominican Republic from education policy discussions because most of the organizations that were in attendance represented residents in Santo Domingo. In reclaiming their position in policy debates, the Coalition proposed that the budget be revised with less emphasize on infrastructure and greater consideration of the human condition (Alcántara, 2013).

This second tenet is an important theoretical contribution because it supports an approach to developing an alternative form of globalization "from below," that is a form of globalization originated from the grassroots level (Brecher, Costello, and Smith, 2000). However, in order for a movement "from below" to gain wide support, effort must be made to involve community members who live where there are no roads or communication signals so that no one is excluded unless they choose to be. In this way, marginality is utopian (Torres, 2009) because striving to reach those who are isolated requires perseverance and commitment to the vision guiding the movement.

The Ability to Initiate Change

The third tenet we add to the theory of marginality is the marginalized have the ability to initiate the creation of a world free of social inequalities. In particular, this tenet extends the fifth tenet of Torres' (2009) theory in that the marginalized are capable of introducing, as well as envisioning and striving for, utopian models of society without neoliberal globalization processes as the driving force of order. We employ this tenet, by examining how the collaboration between the teachers and other organizations, including the Dignified Education Coalition, was fundamental in the success of the "4% for Education" movement and continues to be important in pursuing the objectives of the "Dignifying the Teaching Profession" campaign.

Through the Dignified Education Coalition, the Dominican Association of Teachers has promoted activities to bring attention to the "Dignifying the Teaching Profession" campaign. For example, on March 15, 2013, the Coalition requested the presence of the general public and organizations at an event called, "Teacher, Count on Me," to recognize the validity of the teachers' demand for increased salaries and debate reasonable forms of mobilization to avoid the suspension of classes due to teacher strikes. Through these types of events, the Dominican Association of Teachers frames education as a public interest and appeals to civil society to support teachers as being worthy of higher pay (Dignified Education Coalition, 2013).

With regards to teachers improving their professional lives, teachers have taken initiative to further their education and advance their professional status by collaborating with non-profit organizations.

In fact, teachers have sought out additional training though educational organizations during the summer and have earned specific training to teach Montessori and pre-school. Additionally, many teachers become involved in projects with non-profit organizations to bring resources to their schools and improve their school's infrastructure. Therefore, teachers are seeking different options to traditional opportunities provided by the government.

Employing our third tenet that recognizes that those in a marginal position have the ability to initiate social change contributes to understanding how teachers have begun the process of social transformation by creating dialogue that encourages participation of civil society and through collaboration with non-profit organizations. Our tenet assumes that agency is utilized to initiate change and that change begins with dialogue that includes all stakeholders. The irony is that the neoliberal globalization processes that have revolutionized technology in the Dominican Republic over the last several years facilitating connections between organizations and teachers across the country can, in theory, be an important factor in transfiguring the current neoliberal context.

DIRECTIONS FOR FUTURE RESEARCH

We maintain a research agenda --critical of a neoliberal form of globalization-- is necessary to empower teachers in the Dominican Republic, resulting in more equitable socioeconomic outcomes. Our attempt to advance this agenda consists of adding three tenets to Torres' (2009) theory of marginality, a theory that can help to achieve the teachers' ultimate goals. These tenets accomplish the following: they establish the position of the poor as important for challenging globalization; they integrate the socially isolated in order to promote solidarity; and, they elevate the marginalized as primary actors in creating a better world. For the purposes of our case study, employing these tenets can help influence public support of the "Dignifying the Teaching Profession" campaign and, in turn, increase pressure for policy changes.

However, it is important to point out that further academic work is necessary to push this agenda forward. First, in the context of our case study, researchers need to identify effective mobilization strategies that help to frame the concerns of the poor in terms of globally-recognized, basic human needs in order to connect with others who are suffering and compel government action (Tsutsui and Shin, 2008).

Second, researchers need to discover context-appropriate methods to involve the socially isolated in social movements to increase the possibility of their voices to be inserted into the discourse on globalization and social progress. Third, researchers need to explore prospects for collaborations between researchers and teachers to approach social issues utilizing insights from theory and praxis. Overall, future research needs to develop these lines of inquiry to contribute to possibilities for the empowerment of marginalized populations in challenging globalization processes.

Identifying Mobilization Strategies in the Dominican Republic

Although the government established "dialogue" as a strategy to work with the teachers to improve their socioeconomic well-being over two decades ago (Vaillant, 2005), teachers claim that their needs, and specifically those of the thousands of teachers living in poverty, are being overlooked (Dominican Today, 2013). Up to this point, the Dominican Association of Teachers has protested via strikes, marches, and demonstrations (Assunção, 2011; Diario Libre, 2013), but their ongoing struggle warrants greater attention to mobilization strategies that, in relation to our first tenet, ensure that the demands of the poor are considered. Research on social movements in the Dominican Republic has described protests (Cassa and Murphy, 1995; Espinal, Morgan, and Hartlyn, 2010), but they have failed to identify effective strategies that ensure that the concerns of the poor are considered by government officials. We know that there are different modes of mobilization (e.g. Prempeh, 2006; Seferiades and Johnston, 2012; Tsutsui and Ji Shin, 2008; Usami, 2009). However, certain strategies may work better than others for teachers in the Dominican Republic when taking into account the country's historical and global context. Identifying potentially successful forms of mobilization in the Dominican Republic would be important for teachers to ensure that the perspective of the poor does not get dismissed by political leaders.

Methods to Involve the Socially Isolated

Dominican civil society has not had significant influence on democratic reforms, despite high levels of civic and political participation (Espinal et al., 2010). The work of Espinal et al. (2010) suggests that *who* participates is what matters most in pressuring policy makers. They suggest increasing the participation of those on the periphery of political parties rather than those heavily involved in order to avoid the effects of political parties exchanging benefits for support, which typically results in the prioritization of private demands over public interests.

As our second tenet in the theory of marginality implies, integrating the socially isolated into social movements would increase solidarity because they would be more likely to promote public instead of private interests since they would have fewer connections to political parties. The challenge for researchers is to identify methods to increase their participation. Previous research underscores social networks (Dixon and Roscigno, 2003; Hyojoung and Bearman, 1997; Klandermans and Oegema, 1987) and technology (Gleason, 2013) as important for providing opportunities for individuals to be incorporated in social movements, but increasing participation through networks and the media is problematic in rural regions of developing countries due to the lack of resources. If contextually-appropriate methods could be identified, then the socially isolated may have a better chance of being included into social movements.

Challenging Globalization through Intellectual Collaboration

Marginalized populations around the world are being exploited and oppressed as a result of neoliberal globalization processes, but there is resistance (Polet, 2004; Prempeh, 2006). Teachers, as well as, indigenous groups, university students, and women are among those actively contesting globalization through social movements (Algranati, Seoane, and Taddei, 2004; Stromquist, 2002; Verger and Novelli, 2010). Scholars also contribute to this resistance by analyzing the pursuits of such groups and suggesting alternatives to neoliberal globalization (Gandin, 2006; Mayo, 2005).

In this way, both scholars and citizens are important for social movements and, following Gramscian thought, have the intellectual capacity to contribute to knowledge (Hoare and Nowell Smith, 1971) that can help improve society. Therefore, researchers must identify how collaborations between scholars and citizens can produce insight that can be used to create social change. Existing research highlights participatory approaches as useful for addressing social issues (Kindon, Pain, and Kesby, 2007; McIntyre 2008), but more studies are needed to highlight how participants can be empowered by these approaches. Regarding our third tenet in the case at hand, collaborative research could help teachers use their knowledge to initiate social change, which is a form of empowerment and step towards reclaiming their dignity.

CONCLUSION

In this chapter, Torres' (2009) theory of marginality was employed to interpret the current situation of disenfranchisement faced by public school teachers in the Dominican Republic in the context of a neoliberal form of globalization. The extended version that we offer -- which incorporates three tenets, pursuing social transformation requires the incorporation of the poor, the marginalized are responsible for integrating others who are socially excluded in transformative social justice learning practices, and the marginalized have the ability to initiate the creation of a world free of social inequalities -- enriches the theory as an analytic tool, and constitutes a frame for understanding how teachers and critical scholars can become proactive figures in contesting global processes of inequality and in developing alternative forms of globalization.

When viewed through the lens of marginality theory, the politics that sustain the economic status quo and marginalize Dominican teachers are understood as merely a historically contingent outcome produced by a specific form of globalization. Accordingly, marginality theory is both empowering and democratic; it empowers the marginalized to become politically engaged to overcome poverty or isolation to strive to implement democratic principles of governance.

Overall, the need for intellectuals in academic and non-academic settings to unite in theory-praxis approaches to social problems is important for addressing the need for teacher empowerment, which is the central argument of this chapter. For the case of public school teachers in the Dominican Republic, teachers and critical scholars should work together in seeking greater understanding of how the issues teachers face affect the wider public. After all, these are communities that can attribute the literacy of the young population to those in the teaching profession.

Teachers were major figures in the success of the "4% for Education" campaign, but it took mobilization of the masses to implement meaningful change. Although the end of the "Dignifying the Teaching Profession" campaign is unforeseen, an important step will be greater intellectual collaboration in developing strategies that appeal to the general public and extend the message of empowerment and democracy to the most forgotten communities of the country.

REFERENCES

Acevedo, C. (2013, June 25). Maestros marcharán hoy por aumento salarial y ejecución 4% asignado a educación. *Hoy*. Retrieved from http://www.hoy. com.do/el-pais/2013/6/25/486854/Maestros-marcharan-hoy-por-aumento-salarial-y-ejecucion-del-4-asignado-a.

Adorno, T. W., Frankel-Brunswick, E., Levinson, D. J., and Nevitt Sanford, R. (1950). *The Authoritarian personality*. New York, NY: Harper and Row.

Applebaum, R. P. and Robinson, W. I. (Eds.). (2005). *Critical globalization studies*. New York, NY: Routledge.

Alcántara, R. (2013, August 22). Educación digna denuncia hay exclusión para pacto educativo. *Hoy*. Retrieved from http://www.hoy.com.do/el-pais/2013/8/22/495157/Educacion-Digna-denuncia-hay-exclusion-para-pacto-educativo.

Algranati, C., Seoane, J. and Tadei, E. (2004). Neoliberalism and social conflict: The popular movements in Latin America. In: F. Polet (Ed.), *Globalizing resistance: The state of struggle* (pp. 112-135). Ann Arbor, MI: Pluto Press.

Assunção, K. (2011, October 10). Movilización internacional demanda que República Dominicana dedique el 4% del PIB a educación. *Coalición Educación Digna*. Retrieved from http://educaciondigna.com/2011/10/10/movilizacion-internacional-demanda-que-republica-dominicana-dedique-el-4-del-pib-a-educacion/.

Atasoy, Y. and Carroll, W. K. (Eds.). (2003). *Global shaping and its alternatives*. Bloomfield, CT: Kumarian Press Inc.

Bernstein, B. (1977). *Class codes and control, volume 3: Towards a theory of educational transmission* (2nd ed.). London, UK: Routledge and Kegan Paul.

Bhagwati, J. N. (2004). *In defense of globalization*. New York, NY: Oxford University Press.

Bourdieu, P. and Passeron, J. (1977). *Reproduction in education, society and culture*. London, UK: Sage Publications.

Bowles, S. and Gintis, H. (1976). *Schooling in capitalist America: educational reform and the contradictions of economic life*. New York, NY: Basic Books.

Brecher, J., Costello, J. and Smith, B. (2000). *Globalization from below: The power of solidarity*. Cambridge, MA: South End Press.

Cassá, R. and Murphy, F. (1995). Recent popular movements in the Dominican Republic. *Latin American Perspectives*, 22(3), 80-93.

Central Intelligence Agency. (2013, August 22). *The world factbook: Dominican Republic*. Retrieved from https://www.cia.gov/library/publications/the-world-factbook/geos/dr.html.

Center of Social and Demographic Studies. (2007). *Dominican Republic: Demographic and health survey 2007*. Santo Domingo, Dominican Republic: Center of Social and Demographic Studies. Retrieved from http://www.measuredhs.com/pubs/pdf/FR205 /FR205.pdf.

Ciudadoriental.org. (2013, June 24). Los maestros dominicanos marcharán hacia el Ministerio de Educación para reclamar subida salarial. *Ciudadoriental.org*. Retrieved from http://ciudadoriental.org/index.php? option=com_contentandview=articleandid=8913:losmaestros-dominica nos-marcharan-hacia-el-ministerio-de-educacionandcatid=132:inicial-basica-y-mediaandItemid=331.

Despertar Dominicano. (2013, July 3). Mañana reaparecerán las sombrillas amarillas en demanda de ejecución del 4% para educación en RD. *Despertar Dominicano*. Retrieved from http://www.despertardominicano. com/noticias/noticias-republica-dominicana/8605-manana-reapareceran-las-sombrillas-amarillas-en-demanda-de-ejecucion-del-4-para-educacion-en-rd.

Diario Libre. (2013, March 19). La huelga de maestros le cuesta al país RD$ 203 millones por día. Diario Libre. Retrieved from http://www.diariolibre. com/noticias/2013/03/19/i375963_huelga-maestros-cuesta-paas-203-millones-por-daa.html.

Dignified Education Coalition. (2013, March 15). Coalición Educación Digna se une y llama a participar en la asamblea magisterial abierta "Maestra Cuenta Conmigo." Dignified Education Coalition. Retrieved from http// educaciondigna.com/category/sala-de-prensa/noticias.

Dixon, M. and Roscigno, V. J. (2003). Status, networks, and social movement participation: The case of striking workers. *American Journal of Sociology*, 108(6), 1292-1327.

Dominican Today. (2013, March 26). Teachers below poverty line, says union head. *Dominican Today*. Retrieved from http://www.dominicantoday. com/dr/local/2013/3/26/47126/Teachers-below-poverty-line-says-union-head.

Espinal, R., Morgan, J. and Hartlyn, J. (2010). Civil society and political power in the Dominican Republic. *América Latina Hoy*, 56, 37-58.

Esposito, L. (2009). Human nature, freedom, and neoliberal rationality: Understanding the total market and the prospects for global democratization. In: J. M. Choi and J. W. Murphy (Eds.), *Globalisation and the prospects for critical reflection* (pp. 20-48). Delhi, India: Aakar Books.

Freire, P. (1970). *Pedagogy of the oppressed.* (M. B., Ramos, Trans.). New York, NY: The Continuum International Publishing Group Inc.

Gajardo, M. (2007). *Dominican Republic: Country case study.* Paris, France: UNESCO. Retrieved from http://unesdoc.unesco.org/Ulis/cgi-bin/ulis. pl?catno=155539andset=522D11B8_0_315and gp=0andlin=1andll=1.

Gandin, L. A. (2006). Creating real alternatives to neoliberal policies in education: The citizen school project. In: M. W. Apple and K. L. Buras (Eds.), *The subaltern speak: Curriculum, power, and educational struggles* (pp. 217-241). New York, NY: Routledge.

Gleason, B. (2013). Occupy wall street: Exploring informal learning about a social movement on twitter. *American Behavioral Scientist,* 57(7), 966-982.

Guba, E. G. and Lincoln, Y. S. (1994). Competing paradigms in qualitative research. In: N. K. Denzin and Y. S. Lincoln (Eds.), *Handbook of qualitative research* (pp. 105-117). Thousand Oaks, CA: Sage.

Habermas, J. (1984). *The theory of communicative action,* vol. 1. (T. McCarthy, Trans.). Boston, MA: Beacon Press.

Hoare, Q. and Nowell Smith, G. (Eds.). (1971). *Selections from the prison notebooks of Antonio Gramsci.* New York, NY: International Publishers.

Horkheimer, M. (1972). *Critical theory.* New York, NY: The Seabury Press.

Horkheimer, M. and Adorno, T. W. (1972). *Dialectic of enlightenment.* (J. Cumming, Trans.). New York, NY: Seabury Press.

Hyojoung, K. and Bearman, P. S. (1997). The structure and dynamics of movement participation. *American Sociological Review,* 62(1), 70-93.

International Labour Organization. (2011). *2011 Labour overview, Latin America and the Caribbean.* Geneva, Switzerland: International Labour Organization.

Jorge, M. (2013, February 25). El 98% de los maestros rechaza aumento de un 20%. *Diario Libre.* Retrieved from http://www.diariolibre.com/noticias/2013/02/25/i372922_los-maestros-rechaza-aumento.html.

Kapoor, Dip (Ed.). (2011). *Critical Perspectives on neoliberal globalization, development, and education in Africa and Asia.* Rotterdam, NL: Sense Publishers.

Kindon, S., Pain, R. and Kesby, M. (Eds.). (2007). *Participatory Action Research Approaches and Methods: Connecting People, Participation, and Place.* New York, NY: Routlege.

Klandermans, B. and Oegema, D. (1987). Potentials, networks, motivations, and barriers: Steps towards participation in social movements. *American Sociological Review,* 52(4), 519-531.

Listin Diario. (2012, August 16). Medina anuncia que a partir del 2013 entregará el 4% del presupuesto a educación. *Listin Diario.* Retrieved from http://www.listindiario.com.do/ larepublica/2012/8/16/243798/ Medinaanuncia-que-a-partir-del-2013-entregara-el-4-del- presupuesto-a.

Marcuse, H. (1964). *One dimensional man.* Boston, MA: Beacon Press.

Martínez Vergne, T. (2005). *Nation and citizen in the Dominican Republic 1880-1916.* Chapel Hill, NC: University of North Carolina Press.

Mayo, M. (2005). *Global citizens: Social movements and the challenge of globalization.* London, UK: Zed Books Ltd.

McIntyre, A. (2008). *Participatory Action Research.* Thousand Oaks, CA: Sage Publications, Inc.

Moya Pons, F. (1998). *The Dominican Republic: A national history.* Princeton, NJ: Markus Wiener Publishers.

Murphy, J. W. (2004). The traditional ontology of development, history, and globalization from below. In: J. M. Choi, J. W. Murphy, and M. J. Caro (Eds.), *Globalization with a human face* (pp. 11-24). Westport, CT: Praeger Publishers.

Office of National Statistics of the Dominican Republic. (2011). *Dynamics of child labor in the Dominican Republic.* Santo Domingo, DR: Office of National Statistics of the Dominican Republic. Retrieved from http://www.ilo.org/ipecinfo/product/viewProduct.do?productId=19015.

Organisation for Economic Co-Operation and Development. (2008). *Review of national polices for education: Dominican Republic.* Paris, France: OECD Publishing. Retrieved from http://www.oecd.org/edu/school/reviewsof nationalpoliciesforeducation-dominicanrepublic.htm.

Pan American Health Organization. (2007, October). *Health systems profile: Dominican Republic.* Retrieved from http://hhidr.org/wp-content/uploads/ 2011/10/USAID-Health-System-Profile-DR-2007.pdf.

Polet, F. (Ed.). (2004). *Globalizing resistance: The state of struggle.* Ann Arbor, MI: Pluto Press.

Prempeh, E. O. K. (2006). *Against global capitalism: African social movements confront neoliberal globalization.* Burlington, VT: Ashgate Publishing Company.

Ruccio, D. F. (2011). *Development and globalization: a Marxian class analysis.* New York, NY: Routledge.

Seferiades, S. and Johnston, H., (Eds.). (2012). *Violent protest, contentious politics, and the neoliberal state.* Burlington, VT: Ashgate Publishing Company.

State Secretary of Education of Education of the Dominica Republic. (1997). *General law of education (66-97).* Retrieved from http://sitios.educando. edu.do/biblioteca/components/com_booklibrary/ebooks/ley_general_educ acion_66-97.pdf.

State Secretary of Education of the Dominican Republic. (2008). *Ten-year education plan 2008-2018.* Retrieved from http://www.educacion dominicana.info/2012/03/plan-decenal-de-educacion-2008-2018.html.

Stromquist, N. P. (2002). *Education in a globalized world: The connectivity of economic power, technology, and knowledge.* New York, NY: Rowman and Littlefield Publishers, Inc.

The Stop CAFTA Coalition. (2007). *DR-CAFTA year two: Trends and impacts.* Retrieved from http://www.stopcafta.org/download-report-dr-cafta-year-two-trends-and-impacts/.

Torres, C. A. (2009). *Education and neoliberal globalization.* New York, NY: Taylor and Francis.

Torres-Saillant, S. and Hernández, R. (1998). *The Dominican Americans.* Westport, CT: Greenwood Press.

Transparency International. (2012). *Corruption perceptions index.* Retrieved from http://www.transparency.org/cpi2012/results.

Tsutsui, K. and Shin, H. J. (2008). Global norms, local activism, and social movement outcomes: Global human rights and resident Koreans in Japan. *Social Problems, 55*(3), 391-418.

Usami, K. (2009). Rethinking political opportunity structure in the Argentine unemployed and poor people's movement. In: S. Shigetomi and K. Makino (Eds.), *Protest and social movements in the developing world* (pp. 134-156). Northhampton, MA: Edward Elgar Publishing, Inc.

Vaillant, D. (2005). *Education reforms and teachers' unions: Avenues for action.* Paris, France: UNESCO.

Worker Rights Consortium. 2008. *Living wage analysis for the Dominican Republic.* Retrieved from http://ciee.typepad.com/files/wrc-living-wage-analysis-for-the-dominican-republic-2.pdf.

World Bank. (2013a). *Dominican Republic.* Retrieved from http://data topics.worldbank.org/Education/Country_Dashboard.aspx?code=dominica n-republicandcntycode=DOM,55.

World Bank. (2013b). *Dominican Republic.* Retrieved from http://data.world bank.org/ country/dominican-republic.

United Nations Human Rights Council. (2008, March 18). *Racism, racial discrimination, xenophobia and related forms of intolerance: Follow-up to and implementation of the Durban declaration and programme of action.* Retrieved from http://daccess-ods.un.org/TMP/5175072.55077 362.html.

Verger, A. and Novelli, M. (2010). 'Education is not for sale': Teachers' unions multi-scalar struggles against liberalizing the education sector. In: B. K. Gills (Ed.), *Globalization, knowledge and labour: Education for solidarity within spaces of resistance* (pp. 80-102). New York, NY: Routledge.

Veltmeyer, H. (Ed.). (2014). *Development in an era of neoliberal globalization.* New York, NY: Routledge.

In: Labor Markets   ISBN: 978-1-62948-662-8
Editor: William E. Grossman   © 2014 Nova Science Publishers, Inc.

Chapter 4

"LEARNING A LIVING"? EUROPEAN UNION LIFELONG LEARNING POLICY: ADVOCATING FOR "EMPLOYABILITY"

Eugenia A. Panitsides MSc., PhD.[*]
Department of Educational and Social Policy,
University of Macedonia, Thessaloniki, Greece

ABSTRACT

In the post-industrial context, investment in Lifelong Learning (LLL) has undoubtedly been acknowledged as a conditio sine qua non for sustainable growth and social stability. Especially within the European Union (EU), since the 1990s, LLL has been regarded as a strategic parameter for building the "most competitive economy in the world based on knowledge". In this context ensuring continual adaptability and employability of the work force, particularly the most vulnerable, and combating skills mismatches, have been among main objectives of EU LLL policy to tackle the challenges emerging from increasing competitiveness in the global market, development of information and communication technologies, the Union enlargement, as well as demographic ageing. The present chapter aims to critically review the development of comprehensive LLL strategies in enhancing employment, combating unemployment and increasing competitiveness of the EU.

[*] Adjunct Lecturer, Department of Educational and Social Policy, University of Macedonia, Thessaloniki, Greece, epantsidou@uom.gr.

Given the aims of the study, Critical Discourse Analysis (Fairclough, 1993) has been employed, systematically exploring relationships of causality between discursive practice and wider social structures and processes. Through an interpretative approach of the political discourse, it sought to define trends and identify interrelations between EU LLL strategies and emerging challenges within the Union, as well as global socio-economic mandates. Findings indicated that high unemployment rates during the mid 1990s led to a rhetoric shift replacing "employment" with "employability", whilst rising global competitiveness and economic crisis in 2008 have brought "flexicurity" to the fore. Hence, LLL has been assigned a strategic role in providing for an "up-to-date" workforce, with a better skills match considered "flexible" enough to adapt to changing labor demands, so as to enable EU remain a strong global actor.

Keywords: Lifelong Learning, European Union, Education policy, Employability

INTRODUCTION

During the 1960s the Human Capital Theory (HCT) shifted emphasis onto lifelong education and training. In detail, Abramovich (1956) first outlined that intangible assets could account for a large portion of productivity over and above tangible capital. Later on the human capital theoretical framework was further elaborated through the works of Schulz (1963) and Becker (1964), advocating that investment in human resources, namely on the development of individuals' skills and knowledge, produces economic benefits for economies, organizations, individuals and society as a whole.

HCT has greatly influenced education and training policies throughout Western countries, while on these grounds education has been re-theoritized as primarily an economic device. In this respect, Lifelong Learning (LLL) has been globally acknowledged as a conditio sine qua non for sustainable growth and social stability, being increasingly seen as a "global commodity"(Green, 2002). However, in the European Union (EU) there has been a significant delay in substantially relating economic development to investment in education.

Although stated in the Treaty of Rome (1957) (Official Journal of the European Union, 2002, article 128) that education is the key variable for economic and social progress of peoples in Europe, and provided for by the Treaties of Maastricht (Official Journal of the European Union, 1992, articles

126-127) and Amsterdam (Official Journal of the European Union, 1997, articles 149-150), it took several years to overtly acknowledge the economic value of education and launch an integrated policy agenda on investment in human resources. A milestone in this policy shift was the Lisbon European Council (Commission of the European Communities, 2000b), inaugurating a strategic framework so as to turn EU into the most competitive economy worldwide, based on knowledge. In this context, ensuring continual "adaptability" and "employability" of the work force, particularly for the most vulnerable, and combating skills mismatches, have been among the main objectives of EU LLL policy to tackle the challenges emerging from increasing competitiveness in the global market, development of information and communication technologies, the Union enlargement, as well as demographic ageing (Commission of the European Communities. 2000a, 2000b, 2001a, 20001b; European Council, 2000).

The present chapter attempts to critically review the development of comprehensive LLL strategies in enhancing employment, combating unemployment, and fostering competiveness and growth in the EU. Given the nature of the study, an interpretative approach of the political discourse was adopted, seeking to define trends and identify interrelations between EU LLL strategies and emerging challenges within the Union, as well as global socio-economic mandates.

METHODOLOGY

The mode of analysis employed to conduct the present study rests within Critical Discourse Analysis approach (Chouliaraki & Fairclough, 1999; Fairclough, 1992, 1995), systematically exploring "often opaque relationships of causality and determination between (a) discursive practices, events and texts, and (b) wider social and cultural structures, relations and processes (Fairclough 1995: 132). Following the constructivist assumption that language is a form of social practice, shaped and informed by wider processes within society in a reciprocal interaction, critical analysis of primary texts, such as white papers, official reports, memoranda and strategies, was conducted, in order to grasp insight into political processes, institutions and systems, and interrelatedness of textual properties and socio-cultural practices.

Fairclough (1992, 1995) outlines three integrated levels of discourse, involving analysis of text, discursive practices (e.g. the process of production and consumption), and social practices (e.g. socio-cultural structures which give rise to the communicative event). In this respect, initially the formal properties of the text were studied identifying nodal points and shifts in discourses over time. At a second level an interpretation of the relationship between text, interaction, and the wider socioeconomic context was attempted.

INSTITUTIONAL DISCOURSES ON LLL

The study of the LLL policy framework in the EU was divided into three phases based on milestones considered to have determined the formulation of political discourse, amid contemporary challenges and constraints. Three periods have been identified: a) 1992-1999, b) 2000-2009, c) 2010-today, each one signifying a shift in policy formulation and/or implementation.

1992 – 1999: The Emergence of LLL as an EU Policy Object

Towards the end of the last century, prevalence of a global market coupled with growing economic competition with the United States of America and Japan, the gradual opening of the Chinese market and the parallel collapse of the communist regimes in Eastern Europe, were among the factors that led to the signing of the Treaty on European Union (EU) (Official Journal of the European Union, 1992), the pillar structure towards unification of the European countries. Additionally, rapid development of Information and Communication Technologies (ICTs) and techno-scientific advancement, together with steadily rising unemployment rates in the Community at the beginning of the 1990s, gave impetus for implementing coherent policies that might enhance EU competitiveness in the global arena (Panitsides, 2008, 2013b). Hence, along with mobility enhancement, enabling the movement of goods, services, people and money across member states (Official Journal of the European Union, 1992), rising interest in investment in human resources steadily emerged.

It should be pointed out that political discourse in the 1990s made explicit reference to the economic value of education and training as a means towards unification, social stability and economic prosperity in the member states (Commission of the European Communities, 1993, 1995; European Council, 1996). Education, however, in a slightly differentiated form, flexible, efficient and accessible (Commission of the European Communities, 1995), introducing a novel modus vivendi focusing on learning through life. In particular two

White Papers were endorsed, on "Growth and Competitiveness" (Commission of the European Communities, 1993) and "Education and Training" (Commission of the European Communities, 1995), along with the establishing 1996 as the "European Year of Lifelong Learning" (Official Journal of the European Union, 1995).

Both White Papers were influenced by HCT, highlighting the regulatory role of investment in education in stimulating growth and market efficiency, while improving employment prospects for individuals in a "knowledge economy", either by ensuring a high level of education and training when entering the labor market or/and by continuous updating of knowledge and skills. The policy rhetoric in the particular texts was informed by the Human Resource Development (HRD) approach, namely a set of systematic and planned interventions providing human resources with the opportunity to learn necessary skills to meet current and future job demands (Nadler & Nadler, 1989), with skilling and re-skilling turning into the norm to meet changing requirements in the labor market.

In this context, some of the main issues in the EU educational policy agenda were put forward in the 1990s, such as accessibility to education and training, recognition of skills, comparability and transferability of qualifications, mobility, as well as development of a European accreditation system. Moreover, the necessity for "basic knowledge" acquisition by all was also introduced, referring to a broad and transferable body of knowledge, including basic and social competences, not only for employability purposes, but for remaining functional amid emerging socio-economic transformations in the "learning society" (Commission of the European Communities, 1993, 1995).

Next to the economic arguments there was also a humanitarian dimension in the political text, advocating for potential effect of LLL on maintaining social cohesion, enhancing democratic institutions and promoting active participation of citizens in a "learning society". Furthermore, LLL was considered to be able to alleviate additional problems that arose in the context of European unification, such as issues of national identity, social justice, tolerance, multiculturalism, human rights and equality. (Commission of the European Communities, 1993, 1995; European Council, 1996; Official Journal of the European Union, 1995).

2000 – 2009: Towards a Supra-National LLL Education Policy

Over the new millennium, awareness of the costs of "non-Europe" intensified cooperation among member states which enabled implementation of a convergence policy (Panitsides, Griva & Chostelidou, 2012). A milestone in education policy during this phase was the Lisbon European Council. Once again, under the impact of socioeconomic internationalization, digital technology advancement as well as demographic transformations, compete-tiveness deficiency and unemployment rise faced by the EU called for reforms apt to reinforce economic effectiveness, promote excellence in knowledge and technology, and enhance social cohesion (Milana, 2012). It is interesting to note that two consecutive enlargements (in 2004 and 2007) and the emergence of new competitors in the global arena, such as China and India, urged the necessity for immediate action. Therefore, investment in human capital emerged as nodal point for EU policies at the Lisbon European Council, setting the maximalistic aim "to become the most competitive and dynamic knowledge-based economy in the world, capable of sustainable economic growth" and providing for strategic goals to strengthen employment, economic reform and social cohesion, referred to as the "Lisbon Strategy" (European Council, 2000). Noting that Europe faces "a quantum shift resulting from globalization and the challenges of a new economy driven by knowledge", the objectives set by the Lisbon agenda focused on two closely interrelated parameters to meet the demands of overall development and economic growth: a) restoring full employment and b) enhancing social cohesion. These two priorities were conditioned by a third variable, accessibility to knowledge throughout lifespan and openness of educational systems, so as to provide equal opportunities for all European citizens to participate in the "knowledge economy" (Commission of the European Communities, 2000a, 2001b; European Council, 2001).

It should be notified that what substantially differentiates this phase of EU policies from the previous decade is that investment in human resources evaded the rhetoric level and became an active policy tool for growth and reform (Field, 2001). Thus, a crucial development in EU education policy has been convergence to a coherent policy framework, implemented though technocratic tools such as, comparable among member states, "indicators" and "benchmarks", while focusing on increasing investment in LLL (Commission of the European Communities, 2001b, 2002, 2003; European Council, 2001, 2003). The convergence mechanism towards strategic goals was provided through the "open method of coordination", functioning as the means to spread best practice and set guidelines and timetables for implementing policies. Hence, even though clearly stated that the Community "fully respects the responsibility of the member states for the content of teaching and the organization of education systems" (Official Journal of the European Union, 1992, 1997), a new era in community collaboration in educational matters was initiated, leading to a "European area of education", practically overriding the principle of subsidiarity (Ertl, 2006; Hingel, 2001).

Consequently, there was a gradual shift to a supranational education policy, which was legitimated under the threat of socio-economic costs in the event of failure of the Lisbon Strategy. As highlighted by the Commission (Commission of European Communities, 2004), "poor implementation of the Lisbon Strategy could have devastating costs for Europe, inhibiting progress and delaying development". Yet, in light of the follow-up on the implementation of the Work programme 2010, existence of serious shortcomings and obvious delays were identified, urging higher and more efficient investment in human resources, development of more effective partnerships between key actors, validation of prior learning and provision of open and attractive learning environments, accessible to all, especially to disadvantaged groups (Commission of European Communities, 2005a).

To this end, in March 2005. the European Council relaunched the Lisbon Strategy, refocusing on growth and employment with emphasis on knowledge, innovation and optimisation of human capital, "Europe's most important asset" (Commission of European Communities, 2005b; European Council, 2005). Furthermore, the issue of developing tools to ensure the transparency of diplomas and qualifications had been a strategic priority throughout the decade (Commission of European Communities, 2006b, 2007a; European Council, 2002; Official Journal of the European Union, 2006b).

However, the end of the decade 2000-2009 found the European Union (EU) amid a severe economic crisis, which was assumed to have accounted for the limited effects of the Lisbon Strategy on growth and employment (Commission of European Communities, 2009, 2010a). What was acknowledged though as the most important achievement of the Strategy was improvement in the pace and quality of reforms at national and European levels, having achieved greater consensus and coordination between Member States (Commission of European Communities, 2010a).

2010 – Today: New Tools, New Challenges

The current decade has started with a global economic crisis which reinforced the strong interdependencies among Member States and has indicated closer cooperation as the only way out of recession. Moreover, further socio-economic and demographic challenges in the EU have been associated with a rapidly aging population, a large number of low-skilled individuals and high rates of youth unemployment. In particular, existence of high rates of low-qualified, mismatches between skills and the labor market, and an aging labor force constitute the major structural challenges of the current decade (Cedefop, 2009, 2012; Commission of the European Communities, 2008, 2012; Muenz, 2007), turning investment in education and training, under a "lifelong"' perspective, into a "wonder drug", a modern "panacea" (Panitsides, 2013).

In light of the poor results of the Lisbon Strategy and the ongoing economic crisis, the Council adopted a new strategic framework for European cooperation in education and training in May 2009 (Official Journal of the European Union, 2009). The new agenda, "Europe 2020", mainly focuses on "smart and inclusive growth", so as to build a smarter, greener and more competitive economy, with new jobs and lower levels of unemployment (Commission of the European Communities, 2009; 2011). It combines strategic long-term objectives with short-term priorities and is built on four pillars: a) lifelong learning and mobility, b) quality and efficiency of education and training, c) equity and social cohesion, and d) creativity and innovation. In order to evaluate the performance of Member States in achieving the above-mentioned abstractly articulated strategic goals, four indicators/benchmarks, have been developed, without being significantly differentiated from those of the preceding decade. These concern fostering LLL, improving the quality and effectiveness of education in promoting social cohesion and active citizenship, fostering innovation, creativity and entrepreneurship (Commission of the European Communities, 2009, 2010a; European Council, 2010; Official Journal of the European Union, 2009).

Hence, effectiveness and efficiency of education and training systems is once again among the strategic priorities of the new agenda, in order, as claimed, to ensure personal, social and professional development of all citizens, as well as economic prosperity and employability (Official Journal of the European Union, 2009). Yet, the central plank in the new decade is mainstreaming the use of a set of "European tools", the necessity of which was first outlined during the period 1992-1999, while their development was initiated during the previous decade (Commission of the European Communities, 1993,1995, 2007a; European Council, 2002; Official Journal of the European Union, 2006b). The main "European tools" that have been developed are: a) the European Qualifications Framework (EQF) and National Qualifications Frameworks (NQF), b) the Europass, c) the European Credit System for Vocational Education and Training (ECVET), d) the European Quality Assurance reference framework for Vocational Education and Training (EQAVET) and e) the European Skills/Competences, qualifications and Occupations classification (ESCO). They are assumed to enable greater convergence of education and training in member states, providing for comparability of knowledge, skills, competences and qualifications, and ensuring transparency, with the ultimate aim to enhance mobility within the EU (Commission of the European Communities, 2011).

The foregoing development focuses on the "translation" of qualifications issued all over Europe, making acquired knowledge, skills and competences more transparent and comparable on the basis of "learning outcomes" (Commission of the European Communities, 2012). They practically form a "lingua franca" that facilitates communication not only between the labor market and education but also between education systems among member states. In this respect, there has been prompted a transition of education systems to paradigmatic models based on learning outcomes (knowledge, skills and competencies) achieved not only through formal, but also non-formal and informal learning, while great emphasis has been put on quality assurance of educational interventions.

The main challenge however of the present decade remains combating rising unemployment rates and skills mismatches, which have brought "Flexicurity" to the fore. The Council adopted the common principles of flexicurity in 2007, comprising four components, flexible and reliable contractual arrangements, active labor market policies, life-long learning, and modern social security systems (Commission of the European Communities, 2007b). However, it is only since 2010 that flexicurity was instilled with "a new momentum", under Europe 2020's flagship initiative "An Agenda for new skills and jobs". Reiterating the importance of implementing flexicurity, as a precondition for achieving "smart, sustainable and inclusive growth", it is stressed that its four components must be significantly strengthened and adapted to the new socio-economic context, enhancing partnership of state with social partners with the aim to modernize labor markets and promote employment through new forms of "flexibility" and "security" (Commission of the European Communities, 2010b).

DISCUSSION

As mentioned earlier, in the post-industrial context, investment in LLL has undoubtedly been acknowledged as a conditio sine qua non for sustainable growth and social stability, accompanied by a "grandiose" policy rhetoric (Nicoll & Edwards, 2004). Within the EU, since the 1990s, LLL has been regarded as a strategic parameter for tackling the challenges emerging from globalization and accelerating advances in science and information technology. In the new millennium, however, LLL has become a contemporary "slogan" for EU education policy, packed in a rhetoric highlighting the returns emanating from investment in knowledge (Panitsides, 2012, 2013a, 2013b). Political discourse has been steadily outlining the socio-economic value of LLL, while the role assigned to it in the "knowledge economy" appears inclusive, stabilizing and developmental: a) inclusive, as assumed to provide equal learning opportunities for all citizens, regardless of socioeconomic status and previous educational background, b) stabilizing, through chances for acquiring or upgrading knowledge and skills, both for integration and remaining in the labor market, as well as for ensuring flexibility to socioeconomic transformations, and c) developmental, through "feeding" the labor market with the right mix of knowledge, skills and competences for sustainable growth..

However, the consensus over LLL as a central plank among policy of many Western governments in the field of education, training and employment seems rather problematic in terms of both conceptual framework as well as empirical grounding. In effect, reality is contrasted with rhetoric as contributions of LLL to economic competitiveness and social inclusion are subject to question (Edwards & Nicoll, 2001). According to Coffield (1999), the rhetoric having been developed over the last decades, that LLL is a wonder drug which, on its own, will solve a wide range of educational, social and political ills is naïve and limited. Most importantly, however, it is diversionary, as it advocates "flexibility" and "employability", legitimating escalating demands of employers, intensification of workloads, retreat from the policy of full employment and reduce of public expenditure on welfare measures (Coffield, 1999). LLL tends to signify part of a strategy through which "active citizens" are mobilized in support of their own destinies, wherein the state acts as a monitor and regulator rather than provider of services (Edwards, 2002). Thus, being a participant in LLL appears, to be mostly promoted as "a moral obligation rather than as an opportunity", with "learning a living" becoming the norm (Biesta, 2006; Walker, 2009; OECD, 2005).

It might be argued that the shift in EU LLL policy from the rhetoric level in the 1990s, towards a convergence education policy in the 2000s and a coordinated implementation of a set of technocratic mechanisms and tools in the current decade, may signify a strategic framework in bringing about structural changes in education and employment patterns, as well as in social security systems, with LLL acting as a "Trojan horse". The "flexicurity" case is an eminent example, interconnecting LLL with "flexible and reliable contractual arrangements", and "modern social security systems". In the same vein, the "European tools" were developed on the premises that they may enhance "mobility" in the EU. According to Cedefop (2012), enhanced mobility may account for the mismatch between skills needs and supply, which appears to have a geographical component, as skills shortages and bottlenecks in high growth areas coexist with areas of persistent high unemployment. The question arises as to how "mobility" and "flexibility" will work in favor of wellbeing of peoples in the EU, is not clarified in the political discourse, with references being confined to the expected economic returns.

With this ongoing political debate on the value of the "-ility" word group (flexibility adaptability, employability mobility and so on), denoting discontinuity and instability, one might wonder if Giddens' (1991) arguments for the vital importance of "ontological security", as a sense of order and continuity in regard to an individual's experiences so as to avoid chaos and anxiety, have any practical implications for policy makers in the EU. What is more, overblown policy statements on widening access, inclusion and social cohesion are practically superficial, as disparities in participation in LLL have been continually growing, in benefit of the "included" and not the "unincluded" ones (Edwards & Nicoll, 2001; Walker, 2009). Thus, it seems to be high time to move beyond the present limitations in LLL practices and develop more ambitious and unambiguous policies for creating economic prosperity and substantial social justice (Coffield, 1999, 2000)

CONCLUSION

The present chapter aimed to critically review the development of comprehensive LLL strategies in enhancing employment and increasing competitiveness of the EU. Through a critical analysis of the political discourse, it sought to identify nodal points and define trends and interrelations between EU LLL strategies and emerging challenges within the Union, as well as global socio-economic mandates. Findings indicated that the dominant discourse in employment and education policy, especially since 2000, has been LLL. However, whereas in the past the field of LLL was predominantly informed by a social justice agenda, the current emphasis is on "learning for earning" in which adult learning is seen as a lever for economic growth. This has inflicted a shift towards individualization of LLL, resulting in a situation where it has ceased to be a right and has instead become the individual's duty and responsibility (Biesta, 2006; Walker, 2009).

In particular, the challenges stemming from high unemployment rates during the mid 1990s led to a policy rhetoric shift replacing "employment" with "employability", whilst rising global competitiveness and economic crisis in 2008 have brought "flexicurity" to the fore. Hence, LLL has been assigned a strategic role in providing for an "up-to-date" workforce, with a better skills match and "flexible" enough to adapt to changing labor demands, so as to enable EU regain its competitiveness and remain a strong global actor.

In this context, LLL has become a contemporary slogan. Slogans tend to suggest meanings intended to encompass the hopes of diverse groups, while they are usually mediated through competing interests (Popkewitz, 1980; Werner, 1991). Whether this particular slogan concerns an attempt to legitimate economic imperialism and retreat of welfare services, or provide for a political tool to enhance employment and ensure a high standard of living for all EU citizens, having made clear that the status quo is no longer an option in the contemporary economy it is for the future to tell, especially under compelling conditions of the current global economic recession.

REFERENCES

Abramovitz, M. (1956). Resource and output trends in the United States since 1870. *American Economic Review, 46,* 5–23.

Becker, G. (1964). *Human capital: A theoretical & empirical analysis with special reference to education.* Chicago: University of Chicago Press.

Biesta, G. (2006). What's the Point of Lifelong Learning if Lifelong Learning Has No Point? On the Democratic Deficit of Policies for Lifelong Learning. *European Educational Research Journal,* 5 (3-4), 169-180.

Cedefop (2009). *Learning amid Crisis. Fact Sheet.* Luxembourg: Publications Office of the European Union.

Cedefop (2012). *Skill mismatch: The role of the enterprise: Research Paper No 21.* Luxembourg: Publications Office of the European Union.

Chouliaraki, L. & Fairclough, N. (1999). *Rethinking Critical Discourse Analysis.* Edinburgh: Edinburgh University Press.

Coffield, F. (1999). Breaking the Consensus: Lifelong learning as social control. *British Educational Research Journal,* 25 (4), 479-499.

Coffield, F. (2000). Lifelong learning as a lever on structural change? Evaluation of white paper: Learning to succeed: a new framework for post-16 learning. *Journal of Education Policy,* 15 (2), 237-246.

Commission of the European Communities (1993). *White Paper on Growth, Competitiveness, Employment: The Challenges and Ways Forward into the 21st Century.* Brussels: COM 700.

Commission of the European Communities (1995). *White Paper on Education and Training: Teaching and learning, towards the learning society.* Brussels: COM 590.

Commission of the European Communities (2000a). *The Lisbon European Council: An Agenda for Economic and social Renewal in Europe.* Brussels: Directorate General Education and Culture.

Commission of the European Communities (2000b). *A Memorandum for Lifelong Learning. European Communities.* Brussels: Directorate General Education and Culture.

Commission of the European Communities (2001a). *Making a European Area of Lifelong Learning a Reality.* Brussels: COM 678.

Commission of the European Communities (2001b). *Concrete Future Objectives of Education and Training Systems.* Brussels: COM 59.

Commission of the European Communities (2002). *European benchmarks in education and training: follow-up to the Lisbon European Council: Communication from the Commission.* Brussels: COM 629.

Commission of the European Communities (2003*). Joint Report on Social Inclusion, summarizing the results of the examination of the National Action Plans for Social Inclusion (2003-2005).* Brussels: COM 773.

Commission of the European Communities (2004). *Delivering Lisbon: Reforms for the Enlarged Union. Communication from the Commission.* Brussels: COM 29.

Commission of the European Communities (2005a). *Progress Towards the Lisbon Objectives in Education and Training: Staff Working Paper.* Brussels: Directorate General Education and Culture.

Commission of the European Communities (2005b). *Working together for growth and jobs – a new start for the Lisbon Strategy: Communication to the Spring European Co*uncil. Brussels: COM 0024.

Commission of the European Communities (2006b). *Efficiency and equity in European education and training systems: Communication from the European Commission to the Council and to the European Parliament.* Brussels: COM 481.

Commission of the European Communities (2007a). *Modernising education and training: a vital contribution to prosperity and social cohesion in Europe: Draft 2006 joint progress report of the Council and the Commission on the implementation of the "Education & Training 2010 work programme".* Brussels: COM 549.

Commission of the European Communities (2007b). *Towards Common Principles of Flexicurity: More and better jobs through flexibility and security. Communication from the Commission.* Brussels: COM 359 final.

Commission of the European Communities (2008). *Demography Report 2008: Meeting Social Needs in an Ageing Society.* Brussels: SEC 2911.

Commission of the European Communities (2009). *Consultation on the future "EU 2020" Strategy: Commission Working Document.* Brussels: Directorate General Education and Culture.

Commission of the European Communities (2010a). *Lisbon Strategy evaluation document: Commission Staff Working Document.* Brussels: SEC 114.

Commission of the European Communities (2010b). *An Agenda for new skills and jobs: A European contribution towards full employment.* Brussels: COM 682 final.

Commission of the European Communities (2011). *Supporting vocational education and training in Europe: the Bruges Communiqué.* Luxembourg: Publications Office of the European Union.

Commission of the European Communities (2012). *Rethinking Education: Investing in skills for better socio-economic outcomes: Communication from the Commission to the European Parliament, the Council, the European Economic and Social Committee and the Committee of the Regions.* Strasbourg: COM 669 final.

Edwards, R. (2002). Mobilizing lifelong learning: Governmentality in educational practices. *Journal of Education Policy,* 17 (3), 353-365.

Edwards, R. & Nicoll, K. (2001). Researching the rhetoric of lifelong learning. *Journal of Education Policy,* 16 (2), 103-112.

Ertl, H. (2006). European Union Policies in Education and Training: The Lisbon agenda as a turning point? *Comparative Education,* 42 (1), 5-27.

European Council (1996). *Council Conclusions of 20 December 1996 on a Strategy for Lifelong Learning.* Brussels: OJ C7/1997.

European Council (2000). *The Lisbon European Council: Presidency Conclusions, 23rd-24th March 2000.* Available at http://www.consilium. europa.eu/cms_data

European Council (2001). *The concrete future objectives of education and training systems: Report from the Education Council to the European Council.* Brussels: 5980/01 EDUC 23

European Council (2002). *The Copenhagen Declaration: Declaration of the European Ministers of vocational education and training, and the European Commission, convened in Copenhagen on enhanced European cooperation in vocational education and training.* Brussels: Directorate General Education and Culture.

European Council (2003).*Council conclusions of 5/6 May 2003 on Reference Levels of European Average Performance in Education and Training (Benchmarks).* Brussels: C 134/02.

European Council (2004). *"Education & Training 2010". The Success of the Lisbon Strategy Hinges on Urgent Reforms: Joint Interim Report of the Council and the Commission on the implementation of the detailed work programme on the follow-up of the objectives of education and training systems in Europe.* Brussels: 6905/04, EDUC 43.

European Council (2005). *Presidency Conclusions: Relaunching the Lisbon Strategy: A partnership for growth and employment.* Brussels: 7619/1/05 REV 1.

European Council (2010). *Council conclusions: A New European Strategy for Jobs and Growth.* Brussels: 17/6/2010.

Fairclough, N. (1992). *Discourse and Social Change.* Cambridge: Polity Press.

Fairclough, N. (1995). *Critical Discourse Analysis: The Critical Study of Language.* London: Longman.

Field, J. (2001). Lifelong Education. *International Journal of Lifelong Education,* 20 (1–2), 3–15.

Giddens, A. (1990). *The Consequences of Modernity.* Cambridge: Polity Press.

Green, A. (2002). The many faces of lifelong learning: recent education policy trends in Europe. *Journal of Education Policy,* 17 (6), 611-626.

Hingel, A. (2001). *Education policies and European governance.* Brussels: Directorate General Education and Culture.

Milana, M. (2012). Globalisation, transnational policies and adult education. *International Review of Education,* 58, 777–797.

Muenz, R. (2007). *Aging and Demographic Change in European Societies: Main Trends and Alternative Policy Options. Discussion Paper No 0703.* Washington, DC: World Bank.

Nadler, L. & Nadler, Z. (1989). *Developing human resources.* San Francisco, Ca: Jossey-Bass.

Nicoll, K. & Edwards, R. (2004). Lifelong learning and the sultans of spin: policy as persuasion? *Journal of Education Policy,* 19 (1), 43-55.

Official Journal of the European Union (1992). *Treaty on European Union.* Brussels: C 191.

Official Journal of the European Union (1995). *Decision No 2493/95/EC of the European Parliament and of the Council of 23 October 1995 establishing 1996 as the "European year of lifelong learning".* Brussels: L 256/45–48.

Official Journal of the European Union (1997). *Treaty of Amsterdam amending the Treaty on European Union, the Treaties establishing the European Communities and certain related acts.* Brussels: C 340.

Official Journal of the European Union (2002). *Consolidated Version of the Treaty Establishing the European Community: The Treaty of Rome 1957.* Brussels: C 325/35.

Official Journal of the European Union (2006b). *Modernising Education and Training: A Vital Contribution to Prosperity and Social Cohesion in Europe. Joint Interim Report of the Council and of the Commission on Progress under the 'Education & Training 2010' Work Programme.* Brussels: C 79/01.

Official Journal of the European Union (2009). *Council conclusions of 12 May 2009 on a strategic framework for European cooperation in education and training ('ET 2020').* Brussels: C 119/02.

Organisation for Economic Co-operation & Development - OECD (2005). *Learning a Living: First results of the adult literacy and life skills survey.* Paris: OECD.

Panitsides, E. (2008). The Lisbon Impact upon Greek Lifelong Educational Policy. In N.P. Terzis (Ed.) *European Unification and Educational Challenges in the Balkan* (pp. 381-386). Thessaloniki: Kyriakidis.

Panitsides, E. (2012). Wider Benefits of adult participation in Lifelong Learning courses. *MENON Journal of Educational Research,* 1, 45-52.

Panitsides, E.A. (2013a). Researching returns emanating from participation in adult education courses: a quantitative approach. *International Journal of Lifelong Education,* 1-20, DOI:+10.1080/02601370.2012.753123.

Panitsides, E.A. (2013b). *Lifelong Education: A modern "Panacea"? Wider private and social benefits.* Thessaloniki: University of Macedonia Press (in Greek).

Panitsides, E., Griva, E. & Chostelidou, D. (2012). European Union Policies on Lifelong Learning: In between competitiveness enhancement and social stability reinforcement. *Procedia Social and Behavioral Sciences,* 46, 548 – 553.

Popkewitz, T. (1980). Global education as a slogan system. *Curriculum Inquiry,* 10 (3), 303-316.

Schultz, W. T. (1963). *The economic value of education.* New York: Columbia University Press.

Walker, J. (2009). The inclusion and construction of the worthy citizen through lifelong learning: A focus on the OECD. *Journal of Education Policy,* 24 (3), 335-351.

Werner, W. (1991). Defining curriculum policy through slogans. *Journal of Education Policy,* 6 (2), 225-238.

INDEX

A

access, vii, 1, 3, 4, 7, 8, 31, 36, 38, 39, 51, 54, 57, 70, 73, 95
accessibility, 48, 89, 90
accommodations, 45, 48
active transport, 5
activism, 83
adaptability, ix, 85, 87, 95
additional schooling, 72
adjustment, 8, 27
adolescents, 23
adult education, 100
adult learning, 96
adult literacy, 100
adults, 3, 51, 56
advancement, 40, 88, 90
age, 11, 12, 13, 24, 39, 45, 46, 47
agencies, 73
aging population, 55, 92
aging society, 39
agriculture, 46, 68
airports, 44
algorithm, 7
alienation, 64
ANOVA, 11, 19
anxiety, 95
Asian countries, 68
assessment, 20
assets, 9, 86

assimilation, 6
attachment, 50
attitudes, 56
autonomy, 5
awareness, 67, 73, 90

B

background information, 38
Barcelona, vii, 1, 6, 8, 16, 17, 23, 24, 25, 28, 32, 33, 34
barriers, 51, 65, 71, 72, 81
barriers to entry, 51
base, 37, 39, 52, 53, 67
benchmarks, 90, 92, 97
benefits, 7, 36, 38, 40, 43, 48, 50, 51, 54, 58, 64, 65, 70, 76, 86
Bhagwati, 64, 79
brain, 41
brain drain, 41
businesses, 39, 40, 43, 44, 48, 52, 54

C

candidates, 40
capitalism, 64, 67, 68, 82
Caribbean, 81
case study, 26, 65, 75, 81
cash flow, 53
catalyst, 51, 53, 55, 57

cattle, 68
causal relationship, 26
causality, ix, 86, 87
causation, 26
CCA, 7
certificate, 69
challenges, vii, ix, 37, 39, 58, 66, 85, 87, 88, 90, 92, 94, 96
chaos, 95
Chicago, 96
chicken, 46
child labor, 69, 82
children, 14, 18, 30, 70
China, 90
CIS, 33
cities, 26
citizens, viii, 36, 42, 44, 45, 48, 49, 51, 55, 73, 77, 89, 90
citizenship, 92
civil society, 74, 75, 76
class struggle, 4, 30
classes, vii, 1, 2, 71, 74
classification, 22, 24, 93
clients, 40
clothing, 51
collaboration, 74, 75, 78, 91
Colombia, 33
commercial, 46, 49
commodity, 86
communication, ix, 74, 85, 87, 93
communication technologies, ix, 85, 87
community(s), vii, viii, 22, 35, 36, 37, 38, 39, 40, 41, 42, 43, 44, 45, 46, 47, 48, 49, 50, 51, 52, 53, 54, 55, 56, 57, 58, 65, 72, 73, 78, 91
competing interests, 96
competition, 31, 45, 47, 64, 68, 88
competitiveness, vii, ix, 31, 70, 71, 85, 87, 88, 90, 95, 96, 101
competitors, 90
complement, 49
conflict, viii, 2, 79
connectivity, 83
consciousness, 66, 67
consensus, 91, 94

conservation, 54
construct validity, 10
construction, 26, 30, 101
consumption, 87
contradiction, 3
controversial, 42
convergence, 90, 93, 95
conviction, 71
cooperation, 90, 92, 99, 100
coordination, 4, 47, 90, 91
correlation(s), 10, 16, 22, 26, 27, 28, 29, 30
correlation coefficient, 16, 27
corruption, 69
cost, 9, 30, 51
covering, 70
creativity, 3, 92
credentials, 51
critical analysis, 87, 95
cultural norms, viii, 36
cultural practices, 87
cultural tradition, 53
cultural values, 31
culture, 2, 4, 44, 45, 50, 79
curriculum, 6, 30, 69, 101
customers, 40, 46, 55
cycles, vii, 1, 4, 6, 7, 8, 9, 17, 30, 31, 56

D

Darwinism, 3, 31
debts, 68
deficiency, 90
deficit, 39, 41
delusion, 31
democracy, 78
democratization, 80
demonstrations, 76
Department of Education, 85
dependent variable, 3, 20, 26, 28, 29
developed countries, 7
developing countries, 77
diffusion, 5
dignity, 64, 70, 71, 77
direct investment, 42
discontinuity, 95

discrimination, 69, 83
disposition, 18
distribution, 6, 12, 13, 19, 22, 24
diversification, 37, 40, 55
diversity, 4, 56, 66
division of labor, 4
DOI, 100
domestic violence, 69
Dominican Republic, v, vii, ix, 63, 65, 68, 69, 70, 71, 73, 75, 76, 77, 78, 79, 80, 81, 82, 83
dream, 37, 44

E

Eastern Europe, 88
economic activity, viii, 36
economic competitiveness, 94
economic crisis, ix, 86, 91, 92, 96
economic cycle, 39, 56
economic development, 46, 53, 86
economic growth, 90, 96
economic policy, 55
economic power, 83
economic reform, 90
economic relations, 64, 65
economic status, 78
economic transformation, 89
education postsecondary, viii, 2
educational background, 94
educational experience, 8
educational institutions, 65
educational policy, 89
educational practices, 5, 98
educational process, 5
educational sociodemographics, vii
educational system, 4, 5, 8, 90
educators, 70
egg, 40, 46
elaboration, 12, 13, 14, 15, 16, 20, 21, 23, 25, 27, 28, 65
embassy, 73
employability, ix, 85, 87, 89, 92, 94, 95, 96
employers, 36, 39, 41, 55, 94

employment, vii, viii, ix, 1, 3, 6, 18, 22, 23, 24, 33, 36, 37, 38, 39, 40, 41, 42, 43, 44, 48, 49, 50, 51, 52, 53, 54, 55, 56, 57, 59, 61, 85, 87, 89, 90, 91, 93, 94, 95, 96, 99
employment opportunities, 42, 51, 56, 59
employment status, 38, 43
empowerment, 65, 67, 68, 71, 75, 77, 78
energy, 5, 39
enlargement, ix, 85, 87
entrepreneurs, viii, 36, 52
entrepreneurship, 92
environment, 22, 24
equality, 7, 11, 66, 89
equity, 92, 98
ethnicity, 39
EU, ix, 85, 86, 87, 88, 89, 90, 91, 92, 93, 94, 95, 96, 98
Europe, 3, 5, 86, 90, 91, 92, 93, 97, 98, 99, 100
European Commission, 98, 99
European Community, 3, 100
European Parliament, 98, 100
European Union, v, vii, ix, 85, 86, 88, 89, 91, 92, 96, 97, 98, 99, 100, 101
evidence, 11, 13, 14, 16, 17, 18, 20, 21, 24, 53, 59
evolution, 2, 5
exclusion, 8, 79
exercise, viii, 36
expertise, 47
exploitation, 66, 69

F

factor analysis, vii, 1, 2, 3, 10, 22, 26
factories, 68
families, 56, 70
family income, 68
feelings, 48, 58
fidelity, 11
financial, 40, 42, 43, 45, 53, 56, 68
financial stability, 68
financial support, 45
fishing, viii, 35, 46, 49, 52, 55
flexibility, 93, 94, 95, 98

flexicurity, ix, 86, 93, 95, 96
folklore, 50
food, 51, 70
force, ix, 31, 42, 67, 74, 85, 87
formation, 4, 21, 24, 25, 29, 30
framing, 67
France, 81, 82, 83
freedom, 22, 80
full employment, 90, 94, 98
functionalism, 4
funding, 53, 54, 57, 58
funds, viii, 36, 37, 38, 41, 42, 43, 44, 48, 52,
    53, 54, 55, 56, 57, 58

G

GDP, 70, 73
general education, 4, 12
general knowledge, 20, 21, 22, 24, 26
global competition, 52, 57
global economy, 33, 37
global leaders, 64
globalised world, 3
globalization, vii, viii, ix, 1, 3, 5, 7, 31, 35,
    55, 59, 63, 64, 65, 66, 67, 70, 71, 73, 74,
    75, 77, 78, 79, 81, 82, 83, 84, 90, 94
governance, 47, 78, 99
government spending, 43
governments, 37, 41, 42, 43, 45, 49, 52, 54,
    55, 57, 58, 94
grades, 17
grants, 45
graph, 27
grass, 57
grassroots, 45, 73
Greece, 85
Gross Domestic Product, 70
grounding, 94
grouping, 44
growth, 48, 51, 87, 89, 90, 91, 92, 93, 94,
    95, 98, 99
guidance, 3
guidelines, 5, 91

H

habitat, 5
Haiti, 68
health, 70, 79
hegemony, 3
high school, 31, 40, 41, 69
histogram, 19
history, 44, 45, 50, 56, 82
hobby, 47, 52
homogeneity, 24
hospitality, 42, 45, 50, 53
hotel, 44
human, vii, 1, 2, 3, 4, 30, 57, 66, 73, 75, 82,
    83, 86, 87, 88, 89, 90, 91, 100
human capital, 3, 4, 30, 86, 90, 91
human capital theory, 30
human condition, 66, 73
human resources, 57, 86, 87, 88, 89, 90, 91,
    100
human right(s), vii, 1, 3, 83, 89
hypothesis, 5, 10, 15, 22

I

ideal, 67
identity, 8, 10
illiteracy, 69
imperialism, 96
improvements, 54
income, 37, 39, 41, 43, 48, 51, 53, 54, 56,
    58
income replacement, 41
income support, 43, 51, 53, 56, 58
independence, 11, 14, 15, 16, 17, 19, 20, 27,
    68, 69
independent variable, 13, 26
India, 80, 90
indirect effect, 27, 29, 30
individualization, 96
individuals, viii, 35, 40, 41, 43, 49, 50, 56,
    66, 67, 77, 86, 89, 92
industrial revolution, 39

industry(s), viii, 35, 37, 45, 46, 47, 48, 50, 51, 52, 53, 54, 55, 56, 57, 68, 69
inequality, ix, 6, 31, 63, 64, 69, 78
inflation, 9, 10, 27
Information and Communication Technologies (ICTs), 88
information technology, 94
infrastructure, viii, 36, 37, 43, 45, 51, 52, 54, 57, 58, 73, 74
institutions, 5, 73, 87, 89
integration, 94
interdependence, 5
internal consistency, 10, 11, 23
internal validity, 10
internationalization, 90
interrelatedness, 87
interrelations, ix, 86, 87, 95
intervention, 37, 68
investment(s), viii, ix, 7, 36, 37, 41, 42, 48, 51, 53, 54, 55, 56, 57, 85, 86, 87, 88, 89, 90, 91, 92, 94
IRC, 61
Ireland, 37, 43, 59
irony, 48, 75
isolation, 40, 73, 78
issues, 5, 40, 44, 45, 59, 65, 66, 69, 72, 75, 77, 78, 89

J

Japan, 83, 88
job creation, 43, 51
job satisfaction, 19, 20, 21
jobless, 56
jumping, 31
just society, 67

K

knowledge economy, 31, 89, 90, 94
knowledge-based economy, 90

L

labor force, 69, 71, 92
labor force participation, 69
labor market(s), vii, viii, 3, 4, 6, 7, 8, 9, 10, 18, 30, 31, 36, 38, 39, 89, 92, 93, 94
labor relations, 3
labor shortage, 38
labour force, 41, 55, 57
labour market, 40, 56, 57, 59
labour shortages, 42
landscape(s), 50, 54
Latin America, 69, 73, 79, 81
laws, 7, 71
lead, 5, 6, 7, 51, 52, 57
learning, ix, 23, 30, 31, 63, 65, 66, 67, 72, 78, 81, 88, 89, 91, 93, 94, 95, 96, 97, 100
learning environment, 91
learning outcomes, 93
learning society, 89, 97
leisure, 22, 26, 29
leisure time, 26, 29
lens, ix, 63, 78
level of education, 11, 17, 89
lifelong learning, v, ix, 85, 86, 89, 92, 96, 97, 98, 99, 100, 101
light, 70, 91, 92
linear model, 19, 28, 29
Lisbon Strategy, 3, 90, 91, 92, 98, 99
literacy, 78
LLL, ix, 85, 86, 87, 88, 89, 90, 92, 94, 95, 96
loans, 68
local community, 53
local government, 3, 46
love, 43, 45, 47

M

Macedonia, 85, 101
magnitude, 17
majority, 40
man, 2, 4, 11, 18, 82
management, 52

manufacturing, viii, 35, 57, 68
marches, 70, 76
marketing, 50, 57
mass, viii, 5, 36, 44, 54, 57
matrix, 7, 10
media, 71, 77
medical, 50, 53, 70
medical care, 50, 53
membership, 24, 29
methodology, viii, 2
Miami, 63
middle class, vii, 2, 8, 31
migration, 40, 41, 42, 43, 47, 52, 68
minimum wage, 51
Ministry of Education, 69
models, 26, 74, 93
modernization, 68
momentum, 93
multiculturalism, 89
multinational corporations, 64
museums, 45, 46, 47, 48, 50, 53, 55
music, 50

N

national identity, 89
national policy, 5
nationality, 13, 15, 17, 18, 24
natural resources, 57
neoliberalism, 64
nervousness, 57
normal curve, 19
normal distribution, 11, 19, 24
North America, 38
null, 11, 14, 15, 16, 17, 22, 23, 24
null hypothesis, 11, 14, 15, 17, 22, 23, 24
nursing, 40, 58

O

objective reality, 66
obstacles, 40, 66
OECD, 41, 61, 82, 100, 101
officials, 45, 55, 72, 76

openness, 90
operations, 45, 47, 52
opportunities, viii, 4, 7, 8, 22, 24, 29, 30, 31, 36, 37, 40, 41, 52, 53, 56, 57, 65, 74, 77, 90, 94
oppression, 66, 67, 69

P

parallel, 88
parental pressure, 31
parents, 6, 13, 14, 16, 17, 18, 30
participants, 37, 38, 40, 44, 77
path analysis, 26
pathways, 9
peace, 48
perseverance, 74
personal choice, 39
personality, 79
persuasion, 100
pilot study, 37
policy, ix, 3, 4, 36, 37, 38, 41, 42, 43, 49, 52, 61, 65, 73, 75, 76, 85, 86, 87, 88, 89, 90, 91, 94, 95, 96, 99, 100, 101
policy choice, 42
policy makers, 43, 52, 76, 95
policy options, 38
policy responses, 41
political instability, 68
political leaders, 76
political participation, 76
political parties, 76
political power, 80
politics, 49, 56, 67, 69, 78, 82
population, 7, 10, 11, 12, 14, 17, 39, 41, 43, 44, 45, 49, 51, 53, 70, 73, 78
population group, 11
population size, 39
Portugal, 1, 32
positivism, 66
post-secondary institutions, 40, 41
potential benefits, 50
poverty, 65, 69, 70, 71, 72, 76, 78, 80
poverty line, 80
power relations, 65

praxis, 66, 75, 78
pregnancy, 69
preparation, 4, 9, 22, 30
preservation, 45, 50, 54
president, 70, 73
prestige, 4, 22
principal component analysis, 22, 23
principles, 9, 64, 78, 93
private schools, 5
private sector, 57
professional development, 92
profit, 74, 75
project, 7, 64, 81
prosperity, 39, 88, 92, 95, 98
psychometric properties, 10
public awareness, 70
public education, 67, 69
public health, 69
public interest, 74, 76
public investment, 51, 53, 58
public policy, 37, 56, 58
public schools, 4
public sector, 57
public support, 75
Puerto Rico, 69

Q

qualifications, 7, 10, 14, 15, 16, 18, 30, 41, 89, 91, 93
qualitative research, 81
quality assurance, 93
quality of life, 8, 54, 56
questionnaire, vii, 1, 10, 11, 26

R

rash, 53
rate of return, 43
rationality, 80
reality, 31, 36, 38, 41, 55, 56, 57, 94
recession, 92, 96
recognition, 71, 89
recovery, 23

recreation, 54
recreational, 54
reference frame, 93
reform(s), 69, 73, 76, 79, 83, 90, 91
regionalization, 3
regression, vii, 1, 3, 19, 21, 26, 27, 29
regression analysis, 19
regression model, 19, 26, 27, 29
reinforcement, 101
rejection, 10
reliability, 10, 48
remittances, 68, 69
representativeness, 14, 17
reproduction, 2, 3, 4, 5, 6, 8, 9, 65
reputation, 26
requirements, vii, 1, 3, 18, 40, 89
researchers, 75, 76, 77
residual error, 19
residuals, 19
residues, 19
resistance, 77, 79, 82, 84
resources, 2, 9, 49, 69, 74, 77
response, vii, 2, 39
restaurants, 46, 48
restrictions, 19
restructuring, vii, viii, 35, 39, 55
retirement, 40
revenue, 54
rhetoric, ix, 64, 86, 89, 90, 94, 95, 96, 98
risk(s), 38, 50, 52
Romania, 59
roots, 41, 57
rural areas, 37, 40, 49, 50, 54, 55, 56, 58
rural communities, vii, viii, 35, 37, 41, 42, 49, 50, 51, 52, 53, 54, 55, 56, 57, 58, 65, 72
rural people, 40, 42, 49
rural tourism, vii, viii, 36, 38, 50, 51, 53, 54, 55, 58

S

scatter, 19
school, vii, 3, 4, 5, 6, 7, 9, 10, 11, 12, 22, 30, 31, 65, 68, 70, 71, 74, 77, 78, 81, 82

school work, 4
schooling, 5
science, 1, 94
scope, 39, 50
seasonal employment, viii, 36, 53, 56, 57
secondary education, 9
secondary schools, 30
security, 22, 36, 38, 40, 41, 48, 93, 95, 98
self-employed, 51
self-employment, 57
semi-structured interviews, 37
services, 37, 40, 43, 44, 46, 50, 53, 58, 69, 88, 94, 96
shape, 7, 65
shelter, 51
shortage, 47
showing, 13, 47
signals, 74
significance level, 10, 12, 13, 14, 16, 18, 21
signs, 44
skilled workers, 41
small businesses, 53
small communities, 39, 44, 45, 56
social benefits, 43, 49, 58, 101
social capital, 9
social change, 6, 66, 67, 74, 77
social class, 4
social competence, 89
social context, 69
social control, 97
social group, viii, 2, 6
social hierarchy, 6
social identity, 8
social inequalities, ix, 63, 74, 78
social justice, ix, 63, 65, 66, 67, 69, 72, 78, 89, 95, 96
social maladjustment, 8
social movements, 66, 67, 75, 76, 77, 81, 82, 83
social network, 77
social order, 67
social participation, 22, 23, 24, 29, 31
social problems, 69, 78
social sciences, 27
social security, 93, 95

social status, 7, 8, 36
social structure, ix, 86
socialization, 2, 22
society, vii, 1, 2, 3, 5, 6, 7, 10, 12, 25, 31, 64, 67, 69, 71, 73, 74, 77, 79, 80, 86, 87
socioeconomic status, 94
sociology, 2
solidarity, 66, 71, 73, 75, 76, 79, 84
solution, 57
Spain, vii, 1, 4, 69
species, 2
speech, viii, 2
spending, 37, 56
spin, 100
Spring, 98
stability, ix, 40, 85, 86, 88, 94, 101
stakeholders, 73, 75
standard of living, 96
state(s), 3, 5, 17, 25, 38, 42, 64, 79, 82, 88, 90, 93, 94
state intervention, 64
statistical inference, 19
statistics, 60
stigmatized, 12
stimulation, 55
stratification, 4
stretching, 54
stroke, 13
structural changes, 95
structural unemployment, 42
structuralism, 4
structure, 7, 9, 22, 30, 65, 81, 83, 88
style, 5
sustainability, viii, 36, 38, 53, 57, 58, 59
sustainable economic growth, 90
sustainable growth, ix, 85, 86, 94
Switzerland, 81
symmetry, 17

T

target, 49
taxpayers, 56
teacher training, 69

teachers, vii, ix, 22, 26, 63, 65, 67, 68, 69,
   70, 71, 72, 73, 74, 75, 76, 77, 78, 83
techniques, 10, 22
technological change, 52
technology, 68, 75, 77, 83, 90
tensions, 5
test statistic, 22
theatre, 45
thoughts, 38
tobacco, 68
top-down, 64
tourism, vii, viii, 36, 37, 42, 43, 44, 45, 46,
   47, 48, 49, 50, 51, 52, 53, 54, 55, 56, 57,
   58, 59, 60, 61, 68, 69
tourism industry, viii, 36, 37, 45, 47, 48, 51,
   52, 54, 55, 56, 57
traditions, viii, 36, 49, 50, 53, 57, 60
training, vii, 1, 2, 3, 4, 6, 7, 8, 9, 11, 14, 16,
   17, 18, 20, 22, 23, 26, 30, 31, 51, 54, 69,
   71, 74, 86, 88, 89, 92, 94, 97, 98, 99, 100
training programs, 4
trajectory, vii, 1, 3, 26, 29
transformation(s), ix, 5, 63, 67, 71, 75, 78,
   90, 94
translation, 7, 93
transmission, 4, 79
transnational policies, 5, 100
transparency, 83, 91, 93
transport, 4, 50, 53
transportation, 40, 54
Treaty of Amsterdam, 100
Treaty of Rome, 86, 100
Treaty on European Union, 88, 100

U

UK, 59, 61, 79, 82
unemployed individuals, 42, 51
unemployment, vii, viii, ix, 3, 7, 36, 41, 42,
   68, 69, 85, 87, 88, 90, 92, 93, 95, 96
unemployment rate, ix, 41, 68, 86, 88, 93,
   96
UNESCO, 81, 83
unification, 88, 89
unions, 67, 83, 84

United Nations, 69, 83
United States, 56, 68, 72, 88, 96
universities, 10, 72
university education, viii, 2, 9
updating, 89
upward mobility, 38, 56, 72
urban, viii, 35, 37, 39, 40, 41, 46, 50, 53, 54,
   56, 57, 59

V

validation, 23, 91
valorization, 26
valuation, 19, 23, 24, 25, 29
variables, viii, 2, 10, 11, 12, 13, 14, 15, 16,
   17, 18, 19, 22, 23, 24, 25, 26, 27, 28, 29,
   30
varimax rotation, 22
vein, 95
violence, 3
vision(s), 53, 57, 60, 64, 74
vocational education, vii, 1, 3, 4, 9, 26, 30,
   69, 98, 99
vocational training, 6, 10, 31

W

wages, 69
Washington, 100
waste, 56
wear, 70
welfare, 42, 94, 96
well-being, 58, 76
Western countries, 86
White Paper, 89, 97
wood, 68
work values, vii, 1, 23
workers, 36, 38, 39, 40, 43, 44, 47, 48, 54,
   56, 57, 59, 64, 80
workforce, x, 86, 96
working class, 31
working conditions, 8, 24, 36, 38
workload, 22
World Bank, 69, 70, 83, 100

world order, 4
World Trade Organization, 68
worldwide, 87
worry, 53

xenophobia, 83

yield, 48, 55
young adults, 56
young people, vii, 1, 3, 4, 5, 6, 7, 8, 10, 11,
      12, 13, 17, 18, 19, 20, 22, 23, 24, 26, 30,
      31, 40
young women, 11, 13
youth unemployment, 7, 92